Your College Application

Your College Application

Scott Gelband

Catherine Kubale

Eric Schorr

College Entrance Examination Board
New York

Copies of this book may be ordered from College Board Publications, Box 886, New York, New York 10101. The price is $9.95.

Editorial inquiries concerning this book should be directed to Editorial Office, The College Board, 45 Columbus Avenue, New York, New York 10023-6917.

Library of Congress Catalog Number: 86-71470
ISBN: 0-87447-247-4

Printed in the United States of America

9 8 7 6 5 4 3 2 1

To
our families
and
Penny

Contents

1

Mapping the Application Maze   i

2

Academic Evaluations   15

Personal Statements   33

4

Supporting Documents   57

5

Facts and Myths about
Getting into College   81

The Big Picture   93

Special Situations   105

Getting Ready for the Send-Off 125

Acknowledgments

We could not have written this book without the experience gained in the Office of Undergraduate Admissions at Yale University. We had invaluable help from a support staff made up of loving, dedicated individuals and a group of especially energetic, caring admissions professionals. We also learned a great deal from the talented teachers and guidance counselors who shared their insights with us and, of course, from the thousands of students whose applications provided us with an intimate view of their lives.

We owe special thanks to Walter Manny, whose lively cartoons serve as a reminder of both the human element in the admissions process and the sense of humor with which that process should be approached; to Christopher "Father" Murphy, who always kept us laughing; to Penelope Laurans Fitzgerald, whose loving guidance was an inspiration; and to Margit Dahl for her comments.

We want to thank our families—Carla and Steve Gelband, Joie Gelband, Mary and Bernard Kubale, Caroline Smith, Anne Kubale, Lee and Marvin Schorr, and Susan Schorr—for their endless encouragement and lessons on the finer points of grammar, syntax, and spelling. And, of course, our heartfelt thanks to Carolyn Trager, our editor, for her wisdom, her patience, and the courage she exhibited in taking a chance on three hitherto unpublished writers.

1

Mapping the Application Maze

The Student's Plight

It's Sunday. The application must be postmarked and in the mail tomorrow or the college won't accept it. I've finished my homework. I can't put it off any longer—it's due tomorrow!

What do they want from me? What do I write? What do they want to hear? Why do I have to keep typing my home address and social security number?

Is it true that only class rank and SAT scores matter? What about the yearbook, the newspaper, and the drama club? Will I look just like everyone else?

How can I be different? Am I different? There must be one of me at every high school in the country.

Mom and Dad want me to go to a good college. My older sister wants me to be happy. I don't know what I want. I just want to get in.

I didn't get to see my guidance counselor about my essay topic. Which teachers should I give these recommendation forms to?

What about soccer? Should I write the coach?

I'll fill in my name and address first. Then I'll worry about the rest.

The Admissions Officer's Dilemma

It's Sunday. I've got 30 more applications to read before committee tomorrow. That means 30 kids, 60 essays, 90 recommendations . . .

Will you look at this? This application must be two inches thick! Newspaper clippings, merit badges, photos from France—and what's this? A term paper! I'll read this one later.

Here's one from Crosstown High. Stands twentieth in her class. SATs 580 and 620. Achievements in the 600s. Honors Bio, Honors U.S. History, third-year Spanish . . . hmmm, third-year Latin, too. Sports editor of the newspaper, yearbook photographer, treasurer of the Spanish Club, field hockey.

Bio teacher calls her conscientious and caring. Always asks questions, always prepared.

Spanish teacher calls her lively, a leader, enthusiastic, and a real team contributor.

Essay one about hockey. Essay two about her grandfather.

Sounds nice. But who is she? *Who* is Sally? How can I explain to the admissions committee that she is different from anyone else? What can I point to?

And I have 29 more to go.

If you have imagined or feared either of these scenarios, this book is for you. Whether you are a senior nearing the final hour or someone thinking about college for the first time, this book offers a guiding hand through the perils of the application process.

We wanted to write a book to fill a gap we saw in the college application literature, a book that tells you simply what applications are all about. This is not a "how to choose the right college" book. Others have written on that subject. This is not a "how to get into college" book, either. We make no guarantees of this kind.

If you follow our suggestions, we do promise that your application will offer the college a well-substantiated, consistent, and readable package that will faithfully and accurately reflect the many facets of your life.

The next seven chapters will unravel the mystery that shrouds the application. We aim to dispel the rumors and air the ghosts of college applications past, present, and future.

What we offer is a general philosophy for filling out an application, together with a detailed analysis of both individual elements and finished product. Strategies are provided to help you put your best self forward, and advice is given to help you meet the challenge with confidence.

This book is a guide through the two-dimensional maze of paper. It offers the experienced insiders' knowledge of what brings life, the third dimension, to the application process. We explain what each page of an application really asks for and explore how these documents can later weave together to form a representative whole.

We know the pressures of the admissions process from the professional side. We have read the stellar, the warm, the solid, and the weak applications. We have called each other in the middle of the night about a "hot" folder and lamented over the "good" kids who are impossible to remember the next day. We have lived through the deadlines, the committees, the phone calls, and the letters of admission and rejection.

As assistant directors of undergraduate admissions at Yale University for two years, each of us was responsible for managing the entire application and selection process in a specific geographic area. We evaluated applications and presented them before the admissions committee; interviewed prospective students; traveled to secondary schools; led seminars with students, parents, school officials, and alumni; developed programs for spring recruitment; and coordinated the transfer admissions process.

Altogether we visited over 750 schools, interviewed over 2,500 students, and evaluated over 12,000 applications from 50 states and around the world. In our years at the Yale admissions office we learned that there are no perfect applicants, only applicants who use the application wisely. We learned that the application process is humbling, that it is human, that it is personal and revealing. We learned that each piece of paper is only that. You are the one who will shape, color, and enlarge it.

Understanding the College Application

A college application is not just a list of activities or a scorecard of grades. It is an attempt to get to know you. It is an opportunity for you to offer information about your life—the triumphs and disappointments, both personal and public. It is a time to write of thoughts, fears, and fantasies. Colleges seek to put together a community of young people who are alive—who think, create, interact, share, and care. They seek students who will be challenged, who will challenge others, and who will help build a community of interested and interesting scholars.

You are one of these people. You have lived a full life, made choices, distinguished among options. You have become a growing, thinking person unlike any other.

You are not a formula—not one of a stack of playing cards shuffled by a dean of admissions; not the sum of a series of variables or the intersection of a series of coordinates on an admissions chart; not a pile of grades and standardized test scores. Those scores and percentiles are merely markers, signposts of departure, starting points.

What you must do is figure out how to take your many attributes and present them in a compelling fashion to the college of your choice. You have inclinations, attitudes, opinions, and interests. Develop them. Follow them. Explore. Do not try to stack the deck. No one will be fooled.

An application consists of a biographical information sheet, a high school transcript, sometimes an essay or two, a counselor's report, and possibly some recommendations. We will go into a thorough explanation of each ingredient in the application in the chapters to follow, but it is important to state at the outset that you are in complete control of the product that reaches an admissions office.

Many people think that by the time they fill out an application, all that remains in their control is the essay.

6

Not true. You have not relinquished control over the recommendations, the counselor's report, or anything else for that matter. You have not conferred any ultimate power on the school faculty or administration to determine your destiny.

You have the opportunity to orchestrate, to guide, to manage all the aspects of your public and private life in your application. You have control over who receives the documents and what information those documents will provide. You have the power to put it all together so that members of an admissions committee will feel comfortable with the person they have come to know through your application.

Exploring Yourself

Who are you? Where are you going? What have you learned? What have you left behind? What awaits you? What have you enjoyed? What makes you laugh? What makes you cry? What bores you to distraction? What are your plans for tomorrow? Next year? It is not often that you are asked to examine yourself this closely. It is not an easy task. Someone is asking you not only to describe who you are but also to define the environment in which you are situated and the places to which you wish to travel during your lifetime. Someone is asking you to pinpoint emotions and give them names.

If you take the time to stop and think about all the changes you have been through and the choices you have made along the way, you will begin to see yourself as a unique person. You will see a person forged of opportunities gained and lost; of aspirations, goals, and defeats; of environment and education. You will see yourself in many contexts: at school, in the community, at home with your family, alone. Your experiences in each of these environments can be revealing.

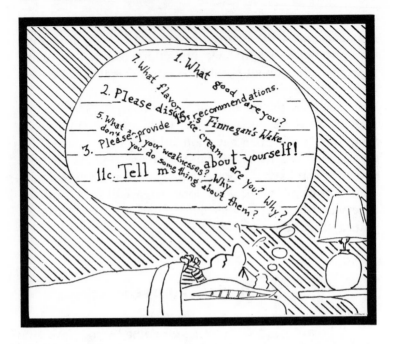

You are a lot of things. Don't sell yourself short. Think about where you were 10 years ago, 10 months ago, 10 days ago. All your experiences help compose the picture of yourself that you will want to describe. Don't be afraid to be human.

If you don't believe in what you're doing, no one else will, either. Take time to think hard about yourself. Write and talk only about those things in which you believe. Don't hesitate to speak about subjects that move you, anger you, or excite you. Be honest with yourself. Don't let others tell you what you should be or what is important to you. Remember, you are an individual. Respect the opinions of others who might be in a better position to see the choices, but remember it is *you* who must live your life. In the end, only you can be genuinely interested in any given topic or activity. Be true to your inclinations, for only then will they be convincing to others.

When you have decided what topics to write about in

your essays and what aspects of your life you will want to discuss in the other application materials, step back and remember to substantiate your claims.

The most confusing application is one that is packed with good information but does not hang together very well. Good ideas, good grades, good scores, good activities, and good recommendations are not as effective as they could be if there are no unifying themes.

You have a lot of information to share. It must be organized properly. It must be presented in a clear, cohesive, creative, and compelling manner. Although you can think of an array of interests, activities, and ideas that are important to you and have shaped you, it is important to be selective. In the end you will want to weave a seamless web where each element of the application leads logically to the next, where documents support each other, and where ideas and ideals are echoed consistently in action.

What Is the College Application All About?

At every high school we visited, someone would invariably ask, "What really goes on in an application? What is it all about?" What seems second nature to those of us who have evaluated applications day in and day out is still a mystery to virtually every student.

Any admissions committee will recognize at least three major areas in a college application: academic, personal, and supporting documents.

The Academic Profile

The first area is the one with which students across the country are all too familiar: the student, or academic, profile. This consists of SAT or ACT or Achievement Test scores, class rank, courses, and grades. These data measure you as a student. They bring to light your accomplishments in the academic arena. Nothing more. Nothing less. An academic profile pegs you as a student, marks your performance in the classroom. It measures your academic achievements and abilities thus far in your school career.

Colleges consider this information because the students they admit will be challenged academically. They want evidence that you can meet and enjoy that challenge. Test scores and class rank are important indicators of your ability and achievement as an individual and in comparison with your peers. They are only the beginning of the story, however, since they are augmented by other parts of the application.

Imagine a college that had the opportunity to admit all the number one students who had the highest SAT scores from all the high schools in the country. The admissions committee could put together a class that certainly would be "brain powerful" and perhaps "scholarly." But would it want to? Where would the so-called human element come from? Who would contribute to the college community at large? Who would stay up until three in the morning musing about literature, laissez-faire economics, and losing football seasons?

We are not saying that those with strong academic profiles are incapable of taking part in activities that make a college thrive outside the classroom. We mean only that colleges are interested in many things about you beyond your potential classroom prowess. Remember, a college can only be as exciting as its students.

The Personal Profile

The second component of an application is the personal profile. Imagine a scale that holds the academic information on one side, the personal profile on the other.

The one acts as a balance to the other, though each is part of the whole.

The personal profile consists of essays, extracurricular activities, and perhaps an interview. This information highlights your personal qualities. While the academic profile reveals you the student, this body of information reveals you the person. It points to your feelings and interests, your reactions and yearnings. It gives you the opportunity to reveal the way you interact in different communities.

The essay topic may vary from college to college. Some institutions will ask you to answer specific questions; others will ask you to fill a blank page with any thoughts you choose. No matter what the format of the question, the underlying intent is the same: admissions committees are seeking to get to know you. They want to know how you spend your time. Tell them what's important to you and why.

The key here is to be yourself. Don't be afraid to say, "I don't know." Don't be afraid to ask questions of yourself, to wonder. The personal profile is your chance to say, "Here I am. Take a look!"

The Supporting-Document Profile

The third and final area is the supporting-document profile. This material brings together the academic and personal aspects of your application. It gives balance to the firsthand account that you provide in an essay and the data that your school record provides. The elements include teacher recommendations, a guidance counselor's report, and supplementary materials.

The supporting documents substantiate and enhance your credentials. They are written by persons who see you in a number of different settings and can assess and describe the extent of your achievements. They bring the application together by providing thoughts and comments about you as a student, as a member of the community, and as an individual.

Supplementary materials are the extra pieces of paper that highlight those aspects of your life not otherwise evident from your application. They are additional letters of recommendation, photographs, artwork, and so forth. Supplementary materials are just that—additional data you choose to provide. Although they are not required, they can prove to be very important in giving balance to the overall picture, but only if they are thoughtfully selected and pertinent.

The strengths of each applicant vary. No two applicants have the same combination of extracurricular strength and academic ability. By and large, an admissions committee is looking for what has come to be described as the well-rounded class rather than the well-rounded student. At one end of a spectrum the committee will find students whose profiles are purely academic; at the other end it will find students whose talents in one extracurricular activity or several activities make them attractive candidates. But the purely academic or the purely extracurricular students will probably make up only a small percentage of those who will be accepted. They will be highly visible in the classroom and the lab, in the auditorium and on the soccer field, but they will not constitute the majority of an entering class.

The majority of a class will consist of students who have a mixture of academic and extracurricular strengths that, for some reason, the admissions committee has found interesting. So don't look around enviously, trying to discover which of your classmates are perfectly well rounded and therefore the ideal applicants. They don't exist. What does exist is the opportunity for you to craft a well-developed, well-planned application that shows you in your best light.

As you plan your application, you should concentrate on how you can best work with your strengths and the materials at hand to convince an admissions committee that you belong in its college's student body. Our goal is to move you away from the particulars and toward developing a completed picture that faithfully reflects your interests and accomplishments. This task will not necessarily be fun. It will probably be exhausting. It will, however, prove rewarding. It may even be exciting.

A Few Words about Financial Aid

When you come to the question on the application about whether or not you will be applying for financial aid, keep the following points in mind:

- The majority of all college students need and receive financial aid. Don't eliminate a college from your list of choices just because of the cost involved. If you qualify for help in meeting college costs, you may get enough outside money to pay for a college that seems beyond your means.

- To get financial aid, you must apply for it. If you plan to apply, be sure to submit your financial aid application and any necessary documents by the required deadline.

Read on. This book is neither a homework assignment nor a lecture. It is an informal guide, a map through the maze of uncertainty that lies between you and the completed application.

2

Academic Evaluations

Some Questions That Could Be Yours

Let's see. . . . They want a copy of my transcript and they want the College Board to send copies of my SAT and Achievement Test scores. All those percentiles. College-bound, non-college-bound. What do they mean? What about the Test of Standard Written English? Does that count? My transcript must look like everybody else's. I have decent grades. I took hard courses, too. But what about those other kids who took the easy way out and got straight A's? They have a higher class rank than I do. How will the colleges know which courses in my school are the hard ones? How will they know that Ms. Hardcastle's section of Honors American History is more work than Ms. Neeley's? I don't seem to have any control over how the admissions office interprets my transcript. My guidance counselor sends it off and that's that.

What Are the Answers?

Relax! There is more fairness in the world of admissions than you may think. The students who take the easy way out probably won't get away with it. Hard work and a sustained effort will certainly bring results.

Your transcript and test scores will convey to an admissions committee your academic strengths and weaknesses. It may seem to you that these are parts of the application over which you have no control, parts of the application that have already been engraved in stone. Granted, you did the engraving—you chose the courses and received the grades—and, admittedly, it is hard to change the surface once it has been polished.

Transcripts and score reports, replete with numbers, rankings, and percentiles, provide an admissions committee with objective, quantitative data. At the same time there is a subjective, qualitative side to these documents, a side that provides you with an opportunity to refinish the stone. Because you are able to select the courses and, to a certain extent, the Achievement Tests you will take, you have an opportunity to reveal to a committee personal strengths that go beyond those measured by numbers and rankings. You actually have more control over your transcript and scores than you may think.

The Transcript

Your Courses and Grades

At its most basic level, your transcript is a list of the courses you have taken and the grades you have received in those courses. (See the example of a typical transcript on page 20.) And yes, admissions officers are very concerned with grades. Your high school grades are among the criteria that indicate your high school performance, which in turn will predict your performance in college. Admissions officers like to see top-notch grades.

There is, however, a distinct difference between having straight A's in easy, or gut, courses (you know what they are: home economics, typing, hygiene) and straight A's in the more demanding honors and advanced courses. Tough courses provide a more compelling transcript. The level of difficulty of the courses counts just as much as the grades. Lots of A's in a not-so-tough course schedule make for a lukewarm impression. An admissions committee would rather see students who challenge themselves, students who are willing to risk receiving a B or a C for the sake of learning. Obviously, if you are receiving all A's in the toughest courses, that's great.

When admissions officers read your transcript, they are asking themselves if you have made the most of the academic opportunities with which you have been presented. In other words, have you taken the most challenging course load possible? They will understand that your course selection depends on the classes available to you. If you attend a small high school that offers only a few honors-level courses, colleges will not expect to see you taking Advanced Placement (AP) classes.

If your high school offers six AP courses, the committee will not expect you to take all six by the time you graduate. You will be expected to take a reasonable number of these courses. If you hate math with a passion but can do well in it, you might consider taking calculus. Beware of "bailout"—forsaking the challenging math and science courses while doing well in English and history or, conversely, forsaking English and history while doing well in math and science. This is a phenomenon that is not looked on favorably by most admissions offices, for it is a signal that you may not be willing to challenge yourself to the fullest.

How do admissions officers know which are the easy courses and which are the hard ones at your high school? Or, for that matter, how do they know whether your high school offers any advanced courses? Part of the job of admissions officers is to familiarize themselves with the schools in their territories. Throughout the fall they visit high schools to talk with students, guidance counselors, and teachers, gleaning what information they can about the quality of the schools and noting differences among them. In addition, most schools have a track record in the admissions office. It is not uncommon for senior admissions officers and deans of admission to be familiar with a wide variety of schools. They have traveled extensively and have good memories.

19

Your College Application

SECONDARY SCHOOL RECORD—TRANSCRIPT

STUDENT INFORMATION			SCHOOL INFORMATION	

Last Name	First Name	Middle Name
Murphy	Penelope	Anne

School Name
Crosstown High School

Home Address
123 Main Street

School Address
456 School Street

Parent or Guardian
Claire Murphy (mother)

School Accredited By ☒ State System ☐ Reg. Accred. Assoc. **School Phone Number**

Previous Secondary School Attended (if any)		Date Left	
		Month	Year

Enrollment in Grades PUBLIC ☒ NON PUBLIC ☐ 9 — 12

Percent Graduates Entering College 4 Yr. Col. 2 Yr. Col. and Other

Date of Birth	Sex	☐ Was Graduated	Month	Year
5/11/69	F	☐ Withdrew	6	87
		☒ Will Be Graduated		

Passing Mark D **Honors Mark (if any)** A, B **LOWEST NUMERICAL EQUIVALENT** A-90 B-80 C-70 D-60

CLASS RECORD
Include Subjects Failed or Repeated

YEAR	SUBJECTS	IDENTIFY LAB TV SEMINAR SUMMER	IDENTIFY HONORS ACCEL. AD. PL. ETC.	MARKS 1ST SEM	MARKS 2ND SEM	CRED OR UNIT	STATE EXAM SCORES
	English 9		3	A	B	4	
	French 2		3	A	A	4	
9	Algebra 1		3	C	B	4	
	Biology		3	B	B		
	Typing		1	A		1	
19 83	Chorus		1	A	A	2	
19 84	Physical Education		1	A	A	2	
	English 10		4	A	A	4	
	French 3		4	A	A	4	
10	Geometry		3	B	B	4	
	Chemistry		4	C	C	4	
	European History		4	B	A	4	
19 84	Chorus		1	A	A	2	
19 85	Physical Education		1	A	A	2	
	English 11		4	A	A	4	
	French 4		4	A	A	4	
11	Algebra 2		3	B	A	4	
	PSSC Physics		4	C	B	4	
	U.S. History		4	A	A	4	
19 85	Chorus		1	A	A	2	
19 86	Physical Education		1	A	A	2	
	AP English*		5			4	
	AP French*		5			4	
12	Trigonometry*		3			4	
	U.S. History-AP*		5			4	
	Spanish 1*		3			4	
19 86	Chorus*		1			2	
19 87	Physical Education*		1			2	
	Driver Education*		1			2	

EXPLANATION OF HONORS COURSES

Please see profile.

RANK IN CLASS BASED ON __6__ SEMESTERS
☒ EXACTLY ☐ APPROX. __23__ IN CLASS OF __339__

FINAL RANK _____ GPA = 4.89

Check Appropriate Rank Information
☐ ALL SUBJECTS GIVEN CREDIT ☒ ALL STUDENTS
☒ MAJOR SUBJECTS ONLY ☐ COLL. PREP. STUDENTS ONLY

Explain Weighting of Marks in Determining Rank

Please see profile.

*indicates course in progress

TEST RECORD

DATE	NAME OF TEST		RAW OR STD SCORE	PERCENTILE SCORE	NORM GROUP	DATE	NAME OF TEST	RAW OR STD SCORE	PERCENTILE SCORE	NORM GROUP
	SAT	Verbal								
		Math								
		Reading								
		Vocabulary								
		TSWE								

20

Your High School's Profile

What if your school is never on an admissions officer's itinerary or is a school from which hardly anyone ever goes to college? Or what if you attend a school that sends very few applicants to the colleges to which you are applying? How can colleges learn about your school? Easily: the school profile. Many high schools attach to their transcripts a sheet of paper that provides colleges with such useful information as the type of community in which the school is located, the racial makeup of the student body, and the percentage of students who go on to pursue higher education.

The profile also provides information about courses and class rank. Thus, if on the transcript the school reports your senior mathematics course as Math 12X, the profile might mention that Math 12X is a typical course in precalculus. In case the profile lacks such information, some colleges will request that your counselor describe in the report the difficulty of your course load relative to that of other members of your class.

You should make a point of asking your guidance counselor or registrar what type of profile (if any) will be sent to the colleges along with your transcript. If you are not satisfied that the document provides an adequate description of either your high school or your course work, have a chat with your guidance counselor, who might be persuaded to incorporate some of your comments into the report. If, after your chat, you remain unsatisfied, you might include with your completed application a statement in which you describe your high school and course load. Be sure, however, that such a statement never becomes the subject of an essay.

Your Class Rank

Along with the list of courses and grades, your class rank will usually appear on the transcript. Class rank sometimes means more to the student than to the admissions office, especially if the rank is unweighted. An unweighted class rank, one that does not take into account the difficulty of your course load, may be less helpful to admissions committees. If your school provides an unweighted rank, admissions officers look closely at your academic program and the school profile in order to determine the difficulty of your course load. An unweighted rank becomes more useful only if there are several students from your school applying to a given college and each student has been taking courses of the same degree of difficulty.

On the other hand, a weighted rank, which gives greater weight to grades in harder courses, is more meaningful; it is a realistic appraisal of your course work. Consider the example of Crosstown High School, whose profile appears on page 23.

Students at Crosstown receive a weighted class rank. There are five levels of courses, and to each grade (A, B, C, D, F) there corresponds a specific number of grade (also called quality) points. For example, an A in a level-5 course is worth 7 points, whereas an A in a level-3 course is worth 5 points. A grade of B in a level-5 course carries the same number of grade points as an A in a level-4 course. To calculate the weighted grade point average (GPA), it is necessary to add the total number of grades, or quality, points and divide by the number of grades. For Penelope Anne Murphy, we arrive at a weighted GPA of 4.89, which places her twenty-third in a class of 339 students. (See transcript on page 20.)

Many schools that use a weighted rank adopt the ranking guidelines developed by the National Association of Secondary School Principals (NASSP) and the American Association of Collegiate Registrars and Admissions Officers (AACRAO). Such systems are well respected by admissions officers. Some schools, such as Crosstown High School in our example above, devise their own ranking system and describe it in the profile.

CROSSTOWN HIGH SCHOOL
CROSSTOWN, U.S.A.
Ann M. Olivarius, Principal
Carolyn Trager, Director of Guidance

The Community: Crosstown High School is the only high school in Crosstown and is one of three high schools in McAllister County. Located approximately 12 miles south of Metrocity, Crosstown (population 29,000) is a residential suburb, inhabited primarily by commuting professionals.

The School: Crosstown High School currently enrolls 1,250 students in grades 9 to 12. The senior class graduating in June 1987 numbers 339; 84 percent of the students are Caucasian, 7 percent black, 9 percent Asian-American. The teaching staff consists of 75 professionals, 72 percent of whom have either master's or doctoral degrees. A guidance staff of 9 counselors helps students make informed career and college decisions.

College Placement: 61 percent of last year's graduates went on to attend 4-year colleges. Another 19 percent decided to pursue a 2-year college education. The remainder entered technical or vocational schools or the armed forces, or sought employment.

Courses Offered: Five levels of courses are offered: Advanced Placement (level 5), Honors (level 4), Above Average (level 3), Average (level 2), Minor (level 1). The level of the course appears on the transcript, in the column to the right of the course title.

Advanced Placement courses are offered in the following subjects: English, U.S. History, Calculus AB, Biology, Chemistry, Physics, French, and Spanish.

Honors courses offered are the following: French 3 and 4, Spanish 3 and 4, PSSC Physics, Chemistry, and Precalculus. The following courses have Honors sections: English 10 and 11, Algebra 1, Algebra 2, Geometry, Biology, U.S. History, and European History.

Computation of Class Rank: A weighted class rank is calculated twice, once at the end of the junior year and again at the conclusion of the senior year. Minor courses—physical education, band, jazz ensemble, yearbook, hygiene, typing, driver education—are not included in the class rank. For each grade there is a corresponding number of grade points, depending on the level of the course:

Grade	Level 5	4	3	2
A	7	6	5	4
B	6	5	4	3
C	5	4	3	2
D	4	3	2	1
F	0	0	0	0

Other schools, particularly those that are either small or "very competitive academically," choose not to rank their students. In those cases, admissions officers look closely at academic programs and grades in order to gain some insight into how a student's performance compares with that of other members of the class.

Still other schools have a compromise solution. They do not give students a specific rank. Rather, students are ranked in deciles, quintiles, or quartiles. To divide a class into deciles means to divide it into 10 groups of equal size. The first decile contains those students in the top 10 percent of the class. The second decile consists of those students in the next 10 percent, or, in other words, those students who rank somewhere between the top 20 percent and the top 10 percent. Similarly, a quintile ranking divides the class into 5 groups, and the first quintile comprises those students in the top 20 percent of their class. A quartile system is made up of 4 groups.

Regardless of the weighting system used, you should be aware that rank, even a weighted rank, in and of itself is but one item on the transcript. It does not tell the whole story of your high school academic career. For example, you had an off year in the ninth grade. Most of your marks were in the mid to the high seventies. You made steady progress and received high eighties in the eleventh grade. Your rank is not as high as that of a fellow student who had high marks from the ninth grade on. If an admissions officer were to look only at your rank and not at your grades, it would not be apparent if your lower rank was the result of a consistent pattern of lower grades or the result of poor performance in just the early years of high school.

The Overall Picture

Because rank does not reveal such important phenomena as improvement trends, admissions officers look at the whole transcript. Your most recent performance (that is, the junior year and the first half of the senior year) gives admissions officers an idea of how you will perform in college, and for this reason they tend to weight this performance more heavily than that of the freshman and sophomore years. Next to a consistently good record, a record that shows steady improvement is a close second.

Class rank also fails to reveal the all-important differences in teachers' grading patterns and preferences. Should Ms. Thomas be a more difficult grader of calculus than is Mr. Heath, your B from Ms. Thomas might well have been an A from Mr. Heath. Your counselor could speak effectively for you in such an instance, perhaps by citing in the recommendation that Ms. Thomas rarely gives high grades.

The best possible transcript you could present to an admissions committee would consist of straight A's in the most advanced program your school had to offer. Not everybody, however, is superstudent, and almost every one of you will have a grade or two or three that you wish were not on the transcript. What about the time your dog ate your history term paper—the one you forgot to make a copy of— and your history grade was a B − instead of a B + ? What about the time you decided to perform badly in a course just to spite your parents? What about the time you fell in love and couldn't be bothered to do your homework for two weeks? What if you or a member of your family had a health problem that kept you from your studies for an extended period of time? Admissions officers are forgiving— up to a point. Excuses for poor performance can never be a substitute for achievement, and those who perform well consistently despite obstacles, amorous or otherwise, will have a distinct advantage.

If you feel pressed to explain your poor performance in a course, you should write a separate letter to that effect, or have your counselor speak for you if you think it appropriate. You should not make such excuses the focus of an essay.

More Than Numbers Can Measure

As plentiful as the wealth of objective information conveyed by the transcript may seem, this document has a substantial subjective side as well. Your transcript tells an admissions committee something about your energy, motivation, and initiative. A transcript full of challenging courses (usually honors or highest-track courses) provides evidence that you are not scared off by tough courses and that you will, most likely, succeed in a competitive academic environment at the college level.

Your courses also provide admissions officers with a sense of your curiosity and ambition. If you have taken an eclectic selection and have achieved well in courses from English to physics, this indicates not only that you are willing to try new things but that you can excel in a wide range of subjects. If, on the other hand, you have taken every science course your school offers and have skipped some of the history or other humanities courses, don't worry. Colleges know that there is often not enough time to do everything.

Your course selection has two components: depth and breadth. Depth indicates how deeply you have delved into any one subject area. For example, if you have followed the math curriculum all the way through calculus, you have achieved great depth of study in this area. Breadth is indicated by your diversity of course selection. If you have taken a wide range of subjects, you will have achieved great breadth of study.

Because you have only a limited amount of time in school, these components, depth and breadth, must be interdependent and occasionally you must sacrifice one for the other. It is impossible to take every course in school, and therefore you will want to explore some subjects at the expense of others. That's fine. You must remember, too, that when you get to college, you'll have the opportunity to explore some more. Most colleges prefer that in high school you acquire a solid foundation in the basics—four years of English, courses in history, science, mathematics, and, more and more frequently, foreign language—and save the experimenting for college.

Tests

Although high schools throughout the country, and the world, vary enormously in size, character, and quality of education, the results of standardized tests are not dependent on the locale in which the tests are given. The very term *standardized* implies uniformity, and standardized tests serve as the sole common gauge by which admissions committees are able to judge candidates from anywhere in the nation (or the world, for that matter). A straight-A transcript from one high school might have been a B or even a C transcript at another, more rigorous institution. A score of 650 on the verbal portions of the SAT taken in Portland, Oregon, is the equivalent of a 650 verbal in Portland, Maine. Therefore, many admissions officers agree that your standardized test scores, in combination with your transcript, will predict your academic performance in college better than your transcript alone will. Because of this enhanced predictive capability and because admissions officers need a standard by which students can be compared with one another, the tests often play a significant role in the admissions process.

Many colleges require either the College Board's Scholastic Aptitude Test (SAT) or the American College Testing Program Assessment (ACT), and some colleges want Achievement Tests, which are also administered by the College Board.

The SAT

The Scholastic Aptitude Test, required by many colleges and universities throughout the United States, is designed to evaluate your aptitude for academic work. The test measures developed verbal and mathematical reasoning abilities related to successful performance in college. It is intended to supplement your secondary school record and other information about you in assessing your readiness for college-level work. The three-hour examination consists of verbal and mathematical sections (two and one-half hours) as well as the 30-minute Test of Standard Written English (TSWE), which measures your facility and familiarity with English usage.

Your score report, a copy of which is forwarded to you and to each of the colleges you specify, contains verbal and mathematical scores on a scale of 200 to 800 and a score for the TSWE based on a 20-to-80 scale. Because the TSWE is not intended to distinguish among students whose command of standard written English is much better than average, the maximum reported score is 60+. In addition, you are provided with various percentile rankings. One gives you an idea of how your scores compare with those of all high school students in the nation. Another allows you to compare your scores with those of college-bound students who took the test. Yet another shows how you compare with students in the state in which you attend high school.

The Achievement Tests

The College Board Achievement Tests are designed to measure your ability in specific subjects. Unlike the SAT, the Achievement Tests are curriculum based and intended to assess outcomes of courses that you have taken recently.

Achievement Test scores, like the SAT-verbal and the

SAT-mathematical scores, are reported on a scale of 200 to 800. You will receive a separate score for each test, as well as an average score for all your Achievement Tests. The percentile rankings will be reported for your Achievement Tests as well.

The ACT

The ACT is required for admission by many schools in the midwestern, western, and southern United States. This group of tests is designed to measure your current level of educational development in four areas—English usage, mathematics usage, social studies reading, and natural sciences reading. It is also intended to assess your ability to perform tasks generally required in college course work.

Your ACT report will contain five separate scores; each will range between 1 and 36—one score for each of the four tests and then a composite score, which is the average of your four scores.

Scores

How big a role do test scores play? Do you have any say about that role? The role of standardized tests in admissions decisions varies considerably from college to college. Some colleges do not require a standardized test for admission but do use it for placement. Other colleges, notably some large state universities, place considerable weight on test scores in making admissions decisions.

Despite the variety of policies regarding tests, it is possible to cull some universal observations about their role in admissions decisions. One such observation is that though standardized test scores are indicators of your academic ability, they are almost always evaluated in relation to other indicators such as your high school transcript.

Sherrie has SAT scores in the 700s and a C – average. Such a situation does not sit very well with an admissions committee, despite the impressive scores that might place her in the 97th percentile at the college to which she is applying. Such a discrepancy indicates that Sherrie is not working up to her potential. Comments from her teachers and counselor might provide an acceptable explanation for the discrepancy—or they might reveal that she is lazy and doesn't work as hard as she should.

Claire, a straight-A student with SAT scores in the upper 400s, does not have quite the same burden of proof as Sherrie because the discrepancy might be explained by some problem that occurred around the time she took the test and interfered with her performance. Positive comments about Claire's schoolwork from teachers might lead the admissions committee to place less weight on her test scores than it would have otherwise.

Another phenomenon common to many admissions offices is that the closer your scores are to the college's medians, the less weight they will carry in the admissions decision. Conversely, the farther away they are from the medians—if they are either extremely high or extremely low—the more attention admissions officers will pay to them. In such cases, however, you must remember that scores constitute only one facet of the decision.

If you have not scored as well as you would like on a standardized test, or as well as you think you could have scored, you may want to take the test again. Some colleges will average your scores; others will take the highest score. Admissions officers generally frown on the results of a fourth or fifth attempt. If, having repeated the test, you remain unsatisfied with the results, do not write to a college to apologize for your scores. If you fell ill during the test or had some other legitimate reason for not doing well, a short note may be appropriate. Otherwise, let bygones be bygones.

In general, you have little control over the role that

most standardized tests play in the admissions process. You can, however, exercise some control over how you appear to a college in the area of the Achievement Tests. Some colleges use the Achievement Tests solely for placement. In other words, if you enroll in the college, your scores will be used to place you in the freshman-year courses that are suited to your academic capabilities. Other colleges use the tests only for admission; still others use them for both admission and placement.

Some colleges require certain Achievement Tests; others permit you to take any three you wish. If, for example, you are applying to an engineering program within a liberal arts curriculum, you will probably be required to take one of the Achievement Tests in mathematics. If the choice is yours, a good overall strategy is to take the tests in the subjects in which you feel you can do your best. Under any circumstances, take them as soon as possible after completing the courses in those subjects.

Do not feel pressed to appear "well rounded" with your Achievement Tests. If you think you can score best on the Biology, Chemistry, and Physics tests, take those three. If you perform better in the humanities than in the math/science area, you might consider taking the tests in English Composition, English Literature, and American History. You need not fear appearing too narrow. Let your transcript show how much academic breadth and depth you have. There is no need to use the Achievement Tests for this purpose.

Before you decide which tests to take, be sure to talk about their content with your teachers, guidance counselor, and any students you know who have already taken the tests. It is important for you to learn how closely your school's curriculum matches that on which you will be tested. Does Mr. Smith's biology class provide you with all you need to know to score an 800 on the Biology Achievement Test? If it doesn't, what extra preparation do you need? Generally speaking, the closer you are to the material, the better you'll do on the test. Even if you received an A in biology last year, you would be wise to pick up your textbook and refresh your memory about mitosis, mitochondria, and the like.

3

Personal
Statements

The Essay

6 6 **I**f I could only write the perfect essay . . . something that will catch their eye. How hard can it be? A topic sentence, five paragraphs, or was it a topic sentence for each paragraph? Maybe I could make it funny. Maybe I should be intellectual: the future of the NATO Alliance. I'd need to do some research for that one. I wonder if I'd have to use footnotes. The perfect essay . . . I know it can be done because I heard about this kid with terrible grades who wrote . . ."

A great essay won't blind the admissions committee to the faults in your application. It can, however, make you stand out in the crowd. Colleges ask for an essay because it helps them understand you as an individual, apart from your grades and test scores. It is an opportunity to show the admissions committee who you are, what's important to you and why. Unfortunately, not all students take full advantage of this.

Many of the essays we read sounded the same. Granted, most of the authors were the same age and were responding to the same question, but where was the individuality? There seemed to be a generic essay for every topic. Whether it was the football team, a trip to France, taking pictures for the yearbook, or singing in the choir, the approach, tone, and substance were similar. To encourage creativity and originality, our office tried a question so broad that there was no hint of what we wanted. But many students still wrote what they thought we wanted to hear. It was frustrating. Here was a chance for the applicants to grab control of the application, and some of them let it slip away.

There is nothing predestined about your essay. You've joined the clubs and you've received the grades. All that is behind you. But the empty space remains. You have a sense that you have some control, that you can still have some impact on the admissions decision. And to a large degree it is true. But do you go out on a limb or do you play it safe? What are they looking for?

Admissions officers want essays that are fresh and original; essays that reflect your interests, ideas, and style; essays that indicate your ability to organize your thoughts and present them in coherent, grammatical form. They don't want to read strained attempts at the perfect essay, the essay you think they want to read. Because the people who read your application have no preconceptions about you, the essay is their chance to get to know you. Let them in. Take chances. Be spontaneous and truthful. The essay should whet their appetite. You want to evoke a response.

Writing an essay is a human exercise. Reading one is too. It's a pleasure to come away from an essay with a sense of someone, with the feeling that you'd like to know that person better. And it's disappointing to come up empty.

The essay also has a more objective purpose: it measures your writing ability. No matter what your topic is, grammar, clarity, style, and neatness are important factors. Obviously, if you are concerned about a low SAT-verbal score or ACT English score, you can offset that weakness with an essay that demonstrates a strong command of the language. Some colleges will also use your essay to determine the level of your freshman English class once you've been admitted.

If your list of extracurricular activities centers around writing, the admissions committee will use the essay to measure your achievements in that realm. The committee will look for the basics: grammar, spelling, and complete sentences. But a clean rendition of the five-paragraph essay isn't enough. Facility, fluidity, and creativity with words and ideas are also important. Don't be afraid to experiment. Use the format that best serves your purpose. The bottom line is that your writing ability will be judged by its effectiveness and not solely by the correct placement of commas.

Choosing a Topic

What should you write about? It's a tough question and one that deserves a lot of thought. An essay has two basic ingredients: the topic and the approach, both of which are equally important. Do you want to write about a conventional topic and take an unconventional approach? Vice versa?

There are an infinite number of topics. The conventional ones usually relate to school activities, trips, and vacations—the more common high school experiences. The unconventional ones reflect personal quirks, ideas, and unique experiences. Play with the possibilities. Observe yourself. Think about what you do, what you think about, whom you spend time with, what interests you, and what bores you.

Think about the various roles you play: at school, among friends, in your family, in the community, and in the classroom. Are they the same? Each arena provides you with possibilities. Don't limit yourself to the most obvious.

Don't feel obligated to write about the activity that takes up the most time. Write about the activity that you find the most intriguing. If spending two hours a week working with the elderly means more to you than twenty hours of swimming practice, write about the work with the elderly. Your essay will be more sincere and more penetrating.

Go beyond the basics. The duties and responsibilities of the various club offices are all too familiar to admissions officers. They understand that a treasurer will be in charge of fund-raising activities. Describing the various techniques used to raise money won't tell them much about you. Think about how the activity has affected you and you have affected it. Explore all the angles.

The time frame of the essay is also open-ended. Don't limit yourself to your years in high school. The future and the past also touch you. Where did your goals come from? What has shaped your life? Who has influenced you? What memory pops up most frequently? Seventeen years provide a wealth of experience. Think about the patterns that emerge from those years.

In a short essay you won't have time to describe all the intricacies of an activity and talk about how it has affected you. So, be careful to choose a topic where the subject won't overwhelm the sentiment. You will want to avoid topics that require a great deal of time to describe what you did or to set the scene. You will want to find a topic that allows you to share your observations, reactions, and reflections. Essentially, this means that an effective topic is one that means something to you.

Go past the activities to the issues, theories, philosophies, and humor. Express your thoughts and reactions, positive and negative. To know you, a person must know not only what you do but what you think. Open up.

You shouldn't avoid topics because they're conventional. If you feel strongly about something, your convictions can bring the conventional to life. But don't cling to a conventional topic because of its familiarity. The topic you choose should challenge you. It should interfere with your thoughts during bio lab and English class. Opening sentences should play through your mind as you try to fall asleep. When this happens, you know that you've found a topic that means something to you.

Choosing a Writing Approach

Choosing a topic is the first hurdle; next you have to decide how you are going to approach it. The approach

38

you choose should reflect your feelings about your topic. Be honest with yourself and the committee. If you've been disappointed by your limited role as tennis captain, don't feel compelled to write an essay about the great effect of your captaincy on the team's season. An essay doesn't have to reflect confidence or indicate complete certainty about your future or your past. Some of our favorite essays were discussions of the fears involved in volunteering in a hospital or in taking up the gavel for the first student government meeting of the year. Sometimes a discussion of fear or anxiety demonstrated a special kind of strength and self-awareness rather than a weakness.

Again, in choosing the approach, consider that the admissions committee wants to learn about you, not the activity. Overly factual or objective approaches meant that we learned more about France, student councils, bands, and newspapers than we ever wanted to know. We came away from too many essays with no better sense of the person we were dealing with than when we started reading. One simple solution is to avoid facts and steer your essay toward observations, reactions, opinions, perceptions, and reflections. Your essay should convey new information or elaborate significantly on what you have already mentioned. If your essay merely rehashes a list of extracurricular activities, you've wasted an opportunity to give the committee new insights. That's frustrating when the committee has only a few pieces of paper from which to extrapolate all the facets of your life.

Admissions officers are human and responsive. They are a sympathetic audience willing to be touched by the interests and thoughts expressed in your essay. We found it easier to be an advocate when we could talk about the applicant as someone we knew, when we felt something or saw something in the application that we could use as a reference point. This reference point often came from an essay. When an essay does nothing more than describe the various tasks involved in holding an office, there is no

39

reference point for admissions officers. They read too many essays that supply only the facts, and those facts begin to run together.

What Makes an Essay Memorable?

Your essay can distinguish you by describing ideas or reactions that are personal and specific. Open yourself up and you will satisfy the curiosity of the admissions officers and give them something by which to remember you. Take an approach that will add a new dimension to your application.

What about the colleges that ask you to respond to a specific essay topic or question: What would you put in a time capsule? With what person in history would you like to eat dinner? Why do you want to go to State University? Why do you want to go to college? There is a perfect answer for these questions, right? Wrong. The colleges are giving you a direction, but they are by no means trying to put a cap on your creativity or individuality. If anything, these kinds of questions present an even greater challenge to your imagination. If Pete Rose has been your hero since you were five, eat dinner with him. It will say more than if you strain to find someone "impressive" whom you studied in history. Admissions committees are interested in your focus, perceptions, and opinions. The specific questions have the same essential purpose as the open-ended questions.

Some colleges have specific requirements for automatic admission: students in the top half or quarter of their high school class, students within a certain range of test scores and grade point averages, and so forth. If you are applying to a college with such a policy and you aren't an automatic admit, you may be asked to provide "any additional information that you think will be helpful." In that particular case, you may want to explain relevant trends or discrepancies in your high school career in a separate statement. Be straightforward and honest. Admissions committees have heard all the excuses. They will also recognize valid explanations. If you think that your strengths or achievements in nonacademic areas deserve consideration, present your case persuasively. You're requesting that an individual exception be made, so present yourself as an individual. In other words, much of the above still applies.

How Long Should the Essay Be?

Many schools will put a specific space limit on the essay. The space limit is there for several reasons. It acts as a constant. Each student is given the same task with equal limits. It forces students to focus and to limit themselves. It also gives an admissions office a realistic chance of getting an admissions decision to you on time. Your application will receive personal attention, but there are also others to be read. As you consider topics and eventually begin to write, concentrate first on the substance. The length will usually take care of itself.

If your essay is effective, the admissions committee will not worry that it is only three-quarters of a page long or a sentence over the space limit. So, first be concerned with what you are saying. If the admissions officer is bored, anything will seem long. If the essay works, the reader will want to learn more about you and will, through the other parts of the application. If you've undertaken more than you can handle, that will be evident as well. When a topic is too big, the space limit will preclude anything more than a surface examination of the issue. Depth is important.

Most important, the freshness and spontaneity of your essay should not be undermined by space requirements. If you've written an essay that pleases you, and it seems a little short, let it be. A gratuitous last paragraph will offset the genuineness of the rest of the essay. Let the substance be your guide.

You also want to be sure that your essay is legible. Some colleges require that you type your essay; others want it written in your own hand. Space limits aren't there to see how small you can write. An admissions officer should never have to struggle to get through to the substance of your essay.

Your one-page essay is your space. Don't waste it. A topic or an approach chosen by your mom, dad, or your best friend won't sound like *your* essay. If you're not engaged in what you're saying, the admissions office won't be, either.

Don't use the space to make excuses for weaknesses in your application. If you had the flu on SAT Saturday, you may want to attach a separate note of explanation, but you shouldn't use the essay to give that information to the committee. If your grades have improved since a weak freshman year, they will see that; it isn't that uncommon. You should use the essay to reveal the positive parts of yourself. If you would like to talk about the reasons for the turnaround in your high school career, you can do so without making excuses for yourself. This doesn't mean that the topic you choose must be cheery and upbeat. Essays that discuss efforts to overcome disappointments and setbacks can be as insightful and telling as essays that discuss achievements.

Writing the Essay

There you are at your desk with this blank piece of paper in front of you. The right essay is still out there somewhere, maybe even in the back of your mind, but not on the tip of your pencil. Now what?

The right essay probably won't happen in one sitting. It will take time, thought, and introspection. Give yourself some time to play with ideas, to search for topics. But eventually you will have to start writing.

If you're struggling and you have the time, try the five-day plan. Each day for five days take a quiet hour to write a draft of an essay. Don't slave over it; all you have to do is fill one page with words. Try five different topics, perhaps in different styles. You might even be inspired to write two pages in one day. Don't be too hard on yourself. Get something down, put it in a drawer, and forget about it. Let the essays sit for the weekend. If a brilliant change comes to mind, note it, but otherwise just let them sit. On Monday read through them all, choose the one you like best, and edit it.

You may want to have someone look at your essay, checking for grammatical and spelling errors, but be sure that the language, ideas, and style are your own. An essay heavily edited by a parent doesn't sound like an essay written by a student.

If, at the end of the five days, you still don't have an essay you like, you might try the five-day plan again. But be careful, don't get too caught up in the search for the ever-elusive perfect essay. Choose a friend who knows you well, whose judgment you trust, to read all five essays and select the favorite. Explain what you've been doing and what you want your essay to say. If your friend finds one that's good, edit the parts that you think ring false or that don't sit well. Your essay should take time and effort, but it shouldn't become an endless quest.

Try not to overedit. An overedited essay becomes stale, stilted. The freshness of the five-day plan is lost when you take the essay apart. If you reacted to the essay positively, the admissions officer reading it will, too. Wrestle with ideas, topics, approaches, and opinions and you will produce an essay that is distinctively yours. If you can learn something from the essay-writing process, the admissions committee will be satisfied that it has learned something as well.

Extracurricular Activities

"I'll never fill this space. All this room for extracurricular activities, and I've heard people ask if they can attach another page. I should have joined the newspaper. The German Club meets only once a month; that would have been easy. Or maybe the basketball team; they say coaches can get anyone in. The Model UN would have been impressive. . . . There's so much room!"

Most students have the same thoughts, the same worries. Take it easy. No one will count your activities. The admissions committee understands that simply the number of activities can't begin to reflect the level of a student's commitment or involvement. The padded résumé is obvious and harmful. The student who joins everything just for show and not out of interest is not an appealing candidate. Interest matters. Commitment matters. You can't join everything. No one has unrealistic expectations.

But that large space stares back at you. It's true that every applicant pool will have one student who will attach extra pages. Don't let that specter haunt you. Students are admitted who can't even begin to fill that space. In the extracurricular portion of the application, the committee is trying to understand how you spend your free time and how much importance you place on each activity. The committee is interested in what is on your list rather than how many activities appear there. Admitted students have varying combinations of extracurricular strength and academic power. That is how a diverse and an interesting class is built. In the extracurricular section, the committee is trying to assess your potential contributions to the class. It is trying to get a sense of you, your talents, your interests, and your level of commitment and expertise.

What counts as an extracurricular activity? Anything that is important to you that takes time, energy, creativity, and responsibility. Begin by jotting down on a notepad every possible activity, hobby, job, and interest that you could put on the list, along with any details or honors that are connected with each activity. You can weed out what isn't significant later when you prepare the final list. The school is a natural starting point, but the arena of extracurricular activities also extends to your community and home. Consider carefully how you've spent your free time over the past three or four years. Think about what has been important to you. Consider who has inspired and instructed you.

In School

The school activities are going to be the easiest for you to remember and identify. They are fairly consistent from school to school, so they can be listed without much explanation. If you were involved for only one year in an activity, don't be afraid to list it as long as it was important to you. You may also want to note if a club or a team folded or lost its funding. One applicant demonstrated a frustration with apathetic classmates by noting, "It folded," "It folded, too," after two of the listed clubs—a simple way to get an important message across.

At Work

Work experience should also be on your list whether or not it is specifically requested in the application. Details of the work experience are just as important as details of any other activity. If you've been promoted twice, say so. Admissions officers also want to know how much time you spend at your job each week. The information will help them assess the impact of working on your grades (if the job eats into homework time) and other

45

extracurricular activities. Understandably, it is difficult to be on a varsity team or in a school play if you work during basketball practice or rehearsals.

In the Community

Although school activities are easily identified, off-campus activities are of equal interest to the admissions committee. These activities may not be so readily familiar to the committee, so you may want to include a sentence or two of explanation. If you are a member of a community committee or organization, you may want to mention its function or purpose. You may also want to indicate how much time is spent on these activities, since this won't be as clear to the committee as is the time involved with the band or the German Club. If you're politically active in the community, in a political party or movement, don't hesitate to indicate your involvement.

Any honor or citation you've received—for example, the rank of Eagle Scout or a community service award—should also be listed. You may want to put these honors under a separate heading so that they're easily visible, or next to the activity to which they are connected.

Hobbies

What about hobbies? It all depends on the time, commitment, and level of interest. Sound familiar? Don't use the occasional knitting of a scarf as filler. Do add a stamp or coin collection that is a continuing and substantial "hobby." You want to avoid distracting the admissions committee. When a committee member asks, "What does he do?" don't make an answer difficult by forcing the committee to discard fluff before finding the substance.

Organizing the List

Once you have a complete list of your activities, you must decide which to list first, which need explanation, and which to leave off the list. Plan the order in which you'll list your activities and think about what the admissions committee will learn from that arrangement. The committee will probably assume that you listed the most important activity first. If you are concerned that your participation in three sports will overshadow your leadership roles in various clubs and committees, arrange your list accordingly. If you run track only to stay in shape, don't group it with your other sports. Place the leadership activities higher on the list.

Quality before quantity. Begin with the activities, honors, and experiences that are most important to you. Don't worry about what sounds most impressive. If you have devoted a great deal of time and energy to an activity, make it readily apparent to the committee. If you include every organization that ever had a meeting announced over the loudspeaker, the committee will wonder what is important to you and what is filler.

How long should the list be? Should you list everything? Be selective. Be honest about your interests, but don't sell yourself short. There will be activities that are important to you and impressive to the committee that don't take a lot of time each week. Every activity listed need not have been a four-year commitment. If you thought only of dance in your freshman year but then burned out, mention it. If you went to three French Club meetings in your sophomore year, don't. The committee is not going to count, and it will become overwhelmed or bored if you list every activity that ever caught your eye.

Consider whether you could hold a conversation with someone about each activity you plan to include on your list. What does it entail? How have you grown from it? What have you learned? What frustrated you about it and why? If there aren't any answers for these questions, you'll want to think twice about listing that activity.

If an activity doesn't sound substantial or important but it keeps you going, put it down. Baby-sitting might not sound like a substantial activity, but if you are the oldest of six children and spend hours each week with your brothers and sisters, list it.

Remember that the person reading your application reads hundreds of these lists each week. Again, a reference point becomes important. A long list can appear unsubstantial if it is difficult for the committee to find any focus or consistency. Therefore, look at each activity individually when you are deciding whether to include it, but also think about the development of interests and trends. Think about connecting those that create a sense of focus.

You also want to make the application as consistent as possible, so consider what others will be writing about you and what activities they are likely to highlight. It will only confuse the admissions committee if you give priority to what sounds impressive and the teacher recommendations mention your deep commitment to an obscure community project that you've put low on your list.

The Overall Impression

This is a good time to start to consider the application as a whole. Think about what kind of impression you would like to leave with the committee. Don't try to change your image. Do consider the information you want them to have. With all the concern about well-roundedness and diversity, the importance of consistency and focus is often underrated. Don't try to create an impression that isn't an honest reflection of your interests and talents. Remember that teachers and guidance counselors will also be talking about your commitment and interests.

In college there is a good chance that studies will force you to limit your activities to one or two strong interests. The committee will be more comfortable adding you to the class if it knows where your interests will lead you. Again, the committee members are not looking for absolutes, but they will be uncomfortable with unknowns and inconsistencies. Choosing your first activity is probably the easiest. It is the second, third, fourth, and even the fifth that make this process difficult. You are going to have to commit yourself. The order in which you list your activities should reveal to the committee their relative importance to you.

Don't ignore time. Although interest and engagement should be your first consideration, if an activity has taken a large chunk of your time each week, mention it. If being photo editor of the yearbook has been a real disappointment, but a 10-hour-per-week commitment, it should be on your list—but not necessarily high on your list.

Give details where it's necessary. Your extracurricular inventory shouldn't be another essay, but sometimes just a title or label won't give the admissions staff enough information. Additional details might include a brief description of the purpose of a club or committee when it isn't self-explanatory, positions or offices held, and personal interests that aren't connected to a club or an organization. If you're sports editor of the school newspaper, but your private writing is the main focus of your creative energy, list both. If you play in the school orchestra, but your private lessons are the source of your growth as a musician, say so. The committee will make some assumptions, but they won't know the level and extent of your involvement unless you tell them.

You'll need to justify, or elaborate on, some of the unique, less easily identifiable activities. One applicant spent hours rebuilding cars. What did that mean? To show us, the student sent before and after pictures of some of the work. It was substantial and creative, and the pictures clued us in.

Don't try to magnify the unsubstantial. Most of the interests, activities, and strengths in your application will speak for themselves.

Bottom line: the admissions officer who reads your application should be able to come up with a few sentences that sum up your extracurricular interests. Your list might look eclectic, but there is probably a theme in there that you can bring out by highlighting the right activities. Don't cut out the activities that won't fit neatly into the picture or theme. Be aware of the message that comes across. The sum total of activities, honors, and interests that you end up with should paint a picture that says something about you. An admissions committee will disregard the number of activities and focus on the level of interest, talent, commitment, and generosity that your activities indicate. Using that list, the committee is going to try to figure out how you spend your time, what makes you tick, and what you'll add to the college community.

The Interview

"No more pieces of paper. They didn't even want my social security number. This is my chance, the only human part of this whole process. If I wow them in the interview, I'm in. Lots of kids from my school couldn't get an appointment. I wonder if that shows a lack of interest. This tie is killing me."

How Important Is It?

Most colleges to which you apply won't require an on-campus interview. Many will not offer it. Most will interview on campus only through the middle of December. Given the large number of applicants, the limited number of appointments available, and the cost of traveling to the colleges for many applicants, most institutions have optional interviews. That should tell you something. An optional interview is not going to be the most important part of the application. The committee can't rely on a piece of information that only a small percentage of the applicant pool will be able to provide. So relax.

This is your chance to present yourself in person. But it's unlikely that the interview will persuade the committee to overlook any weaknesses in your application. Schools will have interviews scheduled in half-hour increments, at most. That's not a lot of time to make up for poor SAT scores or a lack of extracurricular activities. It is plenty of time to establish that you're friendly, articulate, and interested. Don't build it up to be more.

Scheduling

Interviews must be scheduled early. At many colleges the interview schedules are filled by late summer or early fall, especially at those colleges located in natural clusters, such as the eastern schools along I-95 or the California colleges. Plan early. Pick a logical time for your trip and start making appointments. Colleges will understand if you need to cancel because of unforeseen circumstances. They will not penalize you as long as you give them enough warning so that they can fill the slot from their waiting list.

Interviewing is tiring. If you're traveling a long distance, you'll have to balance trying to see as many schools as possible with being alert for the interviews. One way to avoid exhaustion is to interview only at those schools that are realistic options and of real interest to you. Don't let your parents or friends dictate your choice of schools.

Preparation

Read up on the schools that you'll be visiting. Most schools will send you a catalog or bulletin when you call or write for your appointment. If a current catalog is not available, try asking the college for an old one or looking in your high school counselor's office or the local public library. You don't have to do exhaustive research, but in a short interview you don't want to waste time discussing the basics.

If you're familiar with the school, your questions will be probing and will stimulate more interesting conversation. You don't want to raise topics that are already covered thoroughly in the catalog. But if a policy, or the philosophy behind it, confuses you, don't be afraid to ask questions. Again, time is a consideration. Why spend time talking about school size if you can get involved in a discussion of the strengths of possible majors or the accessibility of the faculty?

Think about what you'd like to accomplish in the interview. When we were admissions officers, each of us had a series of questions to draw from so that an interview would last for at least half an hour, but it was much more enjoyable when we could depart from the usual game plan. When you're on your way to the interview, think about the subjects you'd like to discuss, what you'll do when the ball is in your court. A well-placed question can get the interview going in the direction you want. This is your time. The admissions interviewer would like nothing better than a departure from the norm.

What should you wear? Be comfortable. If you haven't worn a tie in three years, don't start now. But don't be overly casual, either. When a student showed up for an interview wearing jeans and a torn shirt, we always wondered what the applicant was trying to prove. If you have a statement to make, verbalize it, don't wear it. Dress in a manner that will allow you to relax and be comfortable, but be respectful.

A Look at Someone Else's Interview

"Please sit down; make yourself comfortable. So you go to Crosstown High. Tell me about the courses you're taking this year."

"Well, I'm taking French four, calculus, American literature, chorus, and American history."

"American literature? What have you read so far this term?"

"The Scarlet Letter, Walden, Billy Budd, The Grapes of Wrath, and *The Sun Also Rises."*

"Tell me, what do you think of the chiastic imagery in *Billy Budd?"*

"The what?"

"Chiastic imagery."

"Uh, what does chiastic mean?"

"Here's a dictionary; look it up."

True story. It happened to Scott at one of his own college interviews. The interview, as you probably guessed, bombed. He was scared to death. Needless to say, he didn't apply to that school.

This isn't a typical scenario. It's everyone's nightmare but rarely the reality. Most interviewers just want to get to know you. They want to find out about you and exchange some thoughts and ideas about their college. When you're handed a tough question, try not to become flustered. Be honest. If you don't understand a question or a word, ask for an explanation. Don't try to discuss something you know nothing about. It's much better to admit you're human than to talk yourself into a hole.

As admissions staff members, we rarely began an interview by asking what book a student was reading or for an opinion about global conflicts. Some of our questions were certainly predictable, but not so difficult that anyone needed to worry about preparing for the questions

ahead of time. Rehearsed answers are like overedited essays—stale.

Try not to look bored. If you're bored, the interviewer probably is, too. Sometimes the chemistry just doesn't work. Don't expect every interview to be great, or even good; often the two personalities involved just don't make that possible. In many ways the interview is the most human part of the application. But that also leads to problems. Some persons just don't mix. Many interviewers are used to drawing out shy people or talking about a variety of subjects. Colleges usually hire recent graduates to do much of their interviewing. This increases the probability of finding some common ground. But every once in a while we would interview students with whom we had nothing in common. We could barely ask enough questions to fill the half hour. It may never happen to you, but don't worry if it does.

Don't expect even the best interview to go over the half-hour mark. Many colleges are now running on 45-minute schedules: 30 minutes to interview and 15 to write up an interview report before starting the next one. Such schedules allow the colleges to interview more students, but this means that time will be limited. The interviewer will be watching the clock carefully. Don't use the length of the interview as a measure of your success.

Checklist of Things to Do

- Maintain eye contact. Catherine recalls one student who stared out the window during the entire interview. It was incredibly distracting.

- Draw the interviewer in. Try to avoid one-sentence answers. Each question is an invitation for conversation. Relate observations and thoughts, not just facts.

- Show engagement and interest. Pay attention to the questions and answers of your interviewer. Nothing is more frustrating to an interviewer than being asked an obvious question and having the student ignore the answer. This is a sure sign of filling time. Trade questions with the interviewer.

- Have fun in the interview.

Checklist of Things Not to Do

- Don't ask the interviewer to compare colleges. The admissions staff is aware of their school's strengths and will be happy to discuss those, but comparisons make an interviewer uncomfortable and are unfair. The choice of a college is a very personal decision. You should do enough research to make the decision yourself based on your needs and interests.

- Don't spend the interview making excuses. The short amount of time you have shouldn't be

wasted explaining poor SATs or how much your
sophomore-year Spanish teacher hated you. The
admissions staff will discover your weaknesses;
you don't have to point them out.

- Don't give the interviewer academic materials
(transcripts, SAT or ACT score reports) unless they
are asked for. Most schools will want to use the
interview to get to know you personally rather
than to review your grades and test scores.

The Pros and Cons of Props

Don't bring materials that are merely security blan-
kets. Many students do little more than clutch the pieces of
paper without any other purpose. These are not effective
props. If you bring photographs or pieces of artwork, be
prepared to talk about them with a novice. Don't expect
your interviewer to have any knowledge about your particular area of interest or to be able to ask even the first right
question. Be ready to lead a discussion of the material.

Sometimes show-and-tell works, sometimes it
doesn't. Props aren't a replacement for conversation.
There should be a purpose behind their use—for example,
your development as a painter, your experiments with
light as a photographer.

Don't make the interviewer go through a long scrap-
book or read articles. The process takes too long and will
only detract from the rest of the interview. There just isn't
time for a thoughtful reaction to such materials.

Most important, relax. Your application is not riding
on the interview. The interview is a friendly, an informa-
tive, and it is hoped, an engaging conversation. Be satisfied
with that.

4

Supporting Documents

"Carla is a hardworking B student. Her work is handed in on time and done with care. She is conscientious, attentive, and willing to contribute to a classroom discussion. Geometry does not seem to be her favorite subject—but she adds to the classroom just the same. I have heard other teachers call her creative. I know she is quite successful socially—gets along well with others."

What you just read is a typical example of one type of supporting document: a teacher recommendation. Other supporting documents are the Guidance Counselor Report and such supplementary materials as an extra letter of recommendation or artwork that you include in your application. Some colleges require supporting documents. Others merely suggest that supporting documents will be accepted. Supporting documents weave together the academic and personal aspects of your application. They give balance to the firsthand accounts that you contribute in an essay and the data that your school record provides.

It's scary to hand a teacher a recommendation form. You can't help but wonder, "What will she say? Will she talk about my strengths and weaknesses? Do I talk enough in class? Do I work well with others?"

Many students believe they have no control over what a teacher or guidance counselor will say about them in a recommendation. Not true! Many students believe they have very little choice as to whom they can select to write these recommendations. Not true! There are a number of things you can do to ensure that a recommendation will echo your sentiments and reinforce the data you have organized in your application. It takes thought. It takes planning. But the final result will be convincing and will reflect your many qualities.

The supporting documents are written by those who know both your academic and your personal strengths. After all, these are the people who have seen you in class, in the halls, on the playing fields, and on the streets. Their recommendations give life to your academic profile and add substance to your personal profile.

We gave an example above of a recommendation. To be honest, it provided very little compelling information. It described a B geometry student who is responsible and hardworking. Nothing special, nothing memorable—simply an endorsement. The teacher didn't seem to know Carla very well at all. Below is an example of a recommendation for the same student that would reinforce other elements of the application and bathe Carla in a favorable light.

"Carla is one of the more interesting students I have taught this year. While it is quite obvious, given her passion for American history and theater, that mathematics is far from her favorite subject, she maintains a steady record of an 86 in my geometry class. She is not afraid to ask questions—rarely will she let a confusing topic lie. I guess I'm content because she adds spark to an early-morning class. I'd rate her overall mathematical ability as average—her spunk and commitment, a gift."

What is the difference between the two? First, it's clear that this teacher knows Carla and likes her. The teacher is up front and honest: Carla is a B student; math is not her favorite subject. But in this example we learn what her other interests are. We learn about commitment, spunk—in short, that Carla is alive and appealing.

How do you end up with the latter kind of recommendation? Who are the people who will endorse your candidacy in the manner you prefer? How do you choose them?

Teacher Recommendations

A teacher recommendation asks a faculty member to make comments about your particular academic skills and, more generally, about your growth and maturity in a social context. It is by nature a subjective document, although it also addresses quantitative and objective data. A typical evaluative request might say:

"Please comment fully on this student's intellectual ability and interests. Any pertinent information that you have to offer regarding the candidate's potential for success in college will be appreciated. Please discuss the student's academic qualifications, special talents (if any), ability to communicate, and level of industry and self-discipline. Thank you."

There are two important areas to consider when you are trying to decide to whom you should give a teacher recommendation form. You must choose a *subject* in which you have some level of skill or proficiency and you must choose the *teacher* who will best be able to highlight your success.

Remember, a teacher recommendation provides an admissions committee with reactions. Teachers react to your candidacy. They react to your skills, your personality, and your inclinations. In building a college community, admissions officers need to gauge such reactions. Teacher recommendations are valuable for this reason.

The object is to choose a teacher who is willing and able to write a full and descriptive recommendation. It's a hard task, so it's important to give the teacher an edge. Choose one who knows you, who has recent experiences with you to draw on. If possible, choose a teacher who seems to have the inclination to write, and give plenty of time for the task. A good recommendation is one that is thoughtfully and carefully written.

Choosing the Subject

Many colleges require at least two academic recommendations. An academic subject, in the eyes of an admissions committee, usually refers to a traditional course: language, literature, mathematics, natural science, history, or social studies. This can include philosophy, religious studies, political science, art history, economics, psychology. Some schools call these courses heavies, solids, building blocks, or majors.

The first rule of thumb: check the college requirements. If the application instructions are not specific, play it safe. Sometimes fully credited subjects like band, choir, newspaper, drama, yearbook, or debate will not be considered core, or academic, courses. It is best to double-check. If no information is readily available, write to or call the college. This will avoid the hassle of sending the proper recommendations after the application deadline has passed.

Not every college requires teacher recommendations. Some welcome supporting documents; others simply remain silent on the subject. Teacher recommendations, if carefully chosen, can be a great boost to your candidacy. When a college doesn't take a stance, don't be shy. Ask whether recommendations are appropriate. Substantiated support from a teacher may make all the difference.

The second thing to consider in choosing the proper subject is the balance of recommendations. When you consider how to organize your application, remember that each piece of information should in some way reinforce some earlier data as well as cast them in a different light. Think about what your choice of subjects will say about you. It should obviously reflect your academic strengths, but it should also reflect your academic interests. (These are not always the same.) What will a pair of history recommendations indicate to an admissions officer as opposed to a history recommendation coupled with a science recommendation? Think about the implications of chemistry paired with physics or French paired with English.

Remember Carla from the opening section of this chapter? What should she submit along with the more forceful of the geometry recommendations? Carla's teacher talked about her passion for American history. An admissions officer would want to see some evidence of this passion. A glowing history recommendation would do the trick. It would provide balance (math/history) and echo the enthusiasm of the first recommendation.

Should you consider a third factor, your choice of major? Many colleges ask you to declare an intended major. If you know that you are going to major in physics, don't hesitate to tell them. In this instance, you should obtain a recommendation from a teacher in that subject to show the admissions committee that you can do the work and that the subject is of genuine interest to you.

On the other hand, if you do not have any idea what your college major will be, don't despair. Unless you are applying to a trade or specialized school, such as engineering or music, it is fine to answer the question with the word *undecided*. It doesn't mean that you are incapable of setting goals. It doesn't mean that you are not mature enough to go to college. It simply means that there are several areas that you will want to explore. In short, if you are decided, back it up. If you are undecided (as most high school students are about future majors), move on to the other considerations that follow.

Fourth, review the grades received in a course or series of courses within a subject. Is it always best to rely on the courses in which you received an A? Not necessarily. Is it flattering to show yourself as the "perfect" student? Or should you seek the comments of a teacher in a course where you have been improving and meeting hurdles?

Imagine that Spanish comes easily to you. You barely have to think to do well on the assignments. In fact, you don't have to pay much attention in class—the book is all you need. The tests come back and you score an easy A. Is this a good subject in which to ask for a recommendation? What about physics? You started out slowly—velocity, acceleration, and rate changes made no sense at all. Then

63

things suddenly came together. Now torque and Einstein are fascinating. Your test scores have been climbing, bringing your average up to an A − . Good choice?

We are not suggesting that you make your choices based on grades or improved efforts alone. We ask only that you consider the variables. Think about your options before you take action.

Fifth, the level of the course is also important. Good grades may have come easily in a first- and second-year language course. But what about the third and fourth years? Remember, the first year of a language or the algebra track of mathematics does not yet show that you have made a sustained commitment to learning a body of material. Introductory courses may not require as much creativity or imagination as more advanced courses, and these are qualities that colleges like to consider.

The sixth item for you to think about: how recent was the course? A subject in which you did well back in your freshman year might not look as good as one you took last semester. What about the memory of a teacher who taught you long ago? Colleges are always interested in growth, potential, and performance. Can a teacher who hasn't seen you in two years write as effectively on these subjects as one who works with you today?

Choosing the Teacher

"Excuse me, um, Mr. McLaughlin? Do you have a minute? I was wondering if you might have the time, I mean be willing to . . . I'm applying to a few colleges, and well, would you be interested in writing, a, uh, writing a recommendation for me? I've got only five of these forms for you to fill out."

In the attempt to decide which teacher to ask to write a recommendation, the first question should be, how well does the teacher know you? Do you shine in a small class?

Are you one of many in a big class? It is important to consider how much contact you have with the teacher before you make any final decisions.

It is a rare occasion in today's school systems to find a teacher who teaches only one course. Most are required to teach several sections of several courses. But their responsibilities do not stop there. Many teachers are also required to coach, sponsor a club, or monitor an activity.

Because there is a good chance that you have been under the careful eyes of a teacher in more than one classroom setting, the second question should be, are there any teachers who have taught you more than once? If so, they may be able to make some astute comments about your growth and intellectual capabilities. A teacher who taught you in both your freshman and junior years has seen your talents and inclinations develop.

"Stephen is a budding English student. When he started my freshman course, he was indifferent, rarely spoke in class, and unfortunately was quite literal and mechanical in his interpretation and analysis. I saw a very different Stephen two years later in the junior course. We read the *Adventures of Huckleberry Finn* in the spring that year. This time Stephen was quite animated. He reached deep into the history of blacks in America and came up with perhaps the boldest look at the character Jim that I have read to date from a teenager. He also speaks up quite regularly in class. He's been a delight."

The third question you should ask yourself is, are there any teachers who have either coached or sponsored an event in which you were involved? Is your history teacher also your tennis coach? Is your French teacher also the Drama Club sponsor? If so, your French teacher will have seen you both in and out of the academic environment and will be able to get closer to the real you, perhaps boosting your candidacy by pointing to both your social and intellectual capabilities.

Do you get along with the teacher? This fourth question is an obvious concern. You may have received a good grade in a course, but if you and the instructor do not see eye-to-eye, the chemistry will not be right. Think for a moment. Do you project any feelings toward a teacher that might affect that person's feelings about you? Have you fought tirelessly and with some glee over a parking space or argued a little too long over a grade with one of the contending teachers? Remember, however, that there is a difference between a teacher with whom you don't get along and one who challenges you in the classroom. If math was easy for you until you ran into the famed Mr. Breslau, who is known for his harsh criticism of student work, don't automatically eliminate him. Criticism doesn't equal disdain or disapproval.

Our fifth query: is the teacher an experienced recommendation writer? How often does he or she write recommendations? Be sure to find someone who is familiar with what a college is looking for in an evaluation, someone who understands that a recommendation is a supporting document, a commentary that must embrace both the academic and the personal sides of you. You may want to consider whether the teacher you are asking has taken an interest in your nonacademic pursuits. Has that teacher congratulated you after a solo performance in a concert or after an election victory? A teacher who takes an interest in your nonacademic pursuits will be more likely to discuss your personal as well as your academic strengths.

The sixth point may be the toughest to gauge: how well does the teacher write? It's good that you got a high grade in a particular course, but it's also important that your teacher can articulately endorse your candidacy and elaborate on your achievements. Admissions officers look for phrases and sentences that epitomize your spirit or abilities. A poorly written recommendation will not do much to further your cause.

How should you assess your teacher's writing ability? Be alert. Be polite. Look at the comments on your papers and report cards. Look in the school paper. Has this teacher written any articles or editorials recently?

It is not the pure writing ability of the teacher that is important but *what* is said about you and how individualized the comments seem. Substance and expression are the focus here; grammar is less important. If English is your German teacher's second language, it's fine to ask for a written recommendation as long as the teacher's thoughts about your achievements can be conveyed in a compelling way.

The Buckley Amendment:
Waiving Your Right to See a Recommendation

The Buckley Amendment concerns your legal claim to see a teacher's recommendation. Quite often a college will ask you to sign your name at the bottom of the recommendation form before you give it to a teacher or counselor. This is nothing more than a waiver. Once signed, it means you waive, or give up, the right to see what a teacher has written about you. You are not required to sign this. If you do sign the waiver, it gives the teacher the flexibility to write freely about you. Teachers tend to be

more honest with words of both praise and criticism when they know that confidentiality will be preserved.

Imagine how you would feel if someone asked you to write a recommendation and you knew that the person might later read it. Would you be as forthcoming about character flaws or weaker skills? Sometimes teachers believe that if they can't balance praise with some criticism, they cannot faithfully recommend a student.

Only if it is imperative that you see your faculty comments should you forgo signing the Buckley Amendment. This is our advice. It will be more difficult to get help from a teacher if you are not willing to entrust him or her with your complete confidence and respect.

Note: If you do not sign the waiver, you will be able to see the recommendations only at the school in which you eventually enroll.

Review the checklists below to be certain you have taken these factors into consideration in choosing the subjects and teachers for your recommendations.

Checklist for Choosing the Subject

- ☐ College requirements
- ☐ Balance or recommendations
- ☐ Choice of major
- ☐ Grade received
- ☐ Level of course
- ☐ Recentness of course

Checklist for Choosing the Teacher

- ☐ How well does the teacher know you?
- ☐ Has the teacher taught you more than once?
- ☐ Has the teacher sponsored an extracurricular activity?

☐ Do you get along?

☐ Does the teacher have experience in writing recommendations?

☐ How well does the teacher write?

Now, after you have juggled all these variables and
found the perfect teacher for you, how are you going to
get him or her to help you out?

Requesting the Recommendation

Here are some rules that will help make the teacher's
job easier.

- Be sure you have all the proper forms.

- Have available a list of your extracurricular activities—your responsibilities and interests both in
and out of school—should the teacher want to use
it in writing your recommendation.

- Prepare a cover letter that simply and explicitly
lists the deadline date for each recommendation.

- Include an addressed and stamped envelope for
each college along with the recommendation
forms.

- If you are planning to sign the Buckley Amendment, be sure you have done so before you turn
over the papers to your teacher.

What you may fear is the hardest part will actually
be the easiest: just screw up your courage and ask a
teacher to recommend you to some schools. It happens

every year. Teachers are used to the idea. If you choose the subjects and teachers carefully by following the suggestions offered above, the recommendations that are eventually submitted will reinforce the strengths of your application. Your academic interests as well as your visible outside activities will be advanced. The recommendations will support your transcript, the thoughts and feelings expressed in your essays, and the interests listed on your extracurricular sheet.

Guidance Counselor's Report

The guidance counselor's report is an integral part of the transcript, or secondary school form. After a counselor has attached your grades, course selection, and standardized test scores, there is usually the opportunity to comment on your abilities. Different colleges request this information in different ways. Some ask specific questions and allow space for an answer in sentence or paragraph form. For example:

"Please list the candidate's honors, awards, and extracurricular activities below and comment on the abilities and interests of the student. In what ways will the candidate contribute to the college environment? Are there any specific problems or talents that merit discussion? Please elaborate."

Other colleges provide a system of check boxes that address particular character traits:

	Excellent	Very Good	Good	Average	Fair	Poor
Motivation						
Independence						
Ability to get along with others						
Initiative						
Creativity						
Academic attitude						
Academic ability						

Still other colleges use a combination of these two formats or simply end the official inquiry after obtaining the numerical data and a blanket endorsement.

What kinds of information can a guidance counselor's report provide? What opportunities are there for you to affect the outcome before the form leaves your hands? How can a guidance counselor help you?

"Joanna stands twenty-third in a class of 250. She plays first trumpet in the marching band and second trumpet in the school orchestra. All her teachers call her witty, charming, and kind. Her academic record speaks for itself. Her good nature is as visible in the community as it is at school. Joanna participates in the county orchestra and also volunteers her time at the local free clinic. One day she will be a doctor, she says. I wholeheartedly endorse her candidacy."

Can you see how the above report could help Joanna's application through the admissions process? In addition to her academic accomplishments, we have learned about her achievements (in music), her interests (in medicine), and her general demeanor (witty and kind). The comment is short but portrays a young woman who is active both in and out of school.

How You Can Affect Your Counselor's Report

Where does the planning fit in? What can you do to ensure that the "right stuff" lands on the page? Let's start by facing the facts. Most of you have absolutely no choice as to who will be your guidance counselor. The first letter of your last name is usually the determining factor.

Typically, a high school guidance counselor is responsible for a group of students; the block is determined by the alphabet (A-G, H-L, M-Q, R-Z). Some counselors track their kids from the ninth through the twelfth grades. Some schools assign counselors by grade so that the students have a new counselor each year. Other schools divide the students by the level of the program in which they are enrolled (standard, honors, or other). In still other schools, the teachers double as counselors.

Whatever the particular situation is at your school, you may think that your guidance counselor doesn't know you very well. Counselors are busy. College counseling may be only one of their responsibilities. They must also worry about class scheduling, discipline problems, truancy. Given the demands on a counselor's time, you may not have had a very close relationship with your guidance counselor up to this point. But don't let this get your spirits down. Your guidance counselor, who may be overworked, is also wise about the world that you share and cares about your future.

Guidance counselors know a lot more about you than you think. Remember, they too are part of the high school community. They read the school newspaper. They see the games, the plays, and the assemblies. Counselors are very good about gathering information on "their kids." They talk to teachers in the faculty lounge and to students in the lunchroom. Department meetings are also a source of information regarding student triumphs and failures.

How do you ensure that your counselor has all the "right" information? Take time to talk to your counselor. Remember, part of the counseling job is to help you plan your college career. Take the initiative. Schedule a short meeting when you have a question. Don't be afraid to stop by the office. Don't be a pest but don't be intimidated, either, by the hustle and bustle of an administrative office.

Once you have chosen the colleges to which you will apply, make an appointment with your counselor. Bring along the proper report forms. It is important to show an interest—and that you mean business.

Go prepared with a full list (on a separate piece of paper) of your extracurricular activities. It is easy for a counselor to write about your interests and activities at school. It's the other interests that will need substantiation. What about all your activities that may be behind the scenes or removed from the school environment? If you play the flute for two hours a day but you don't play in the school orchestra, write it down. If you work ten hours a week at the local grocery store, write it down. If you have been working on an old car since you were 14, write it down. If you have made a decision about an essay topic, it is best to include this on your extracurricular list.

Your counselor will integrate your list of special interests into the report. Give all the information you can on this piece of paper, and the counselor will do the rest. Take the following items to your meeting:

Checklist for Counselor Meeting

☐ All proper forms
☐ Full list of extracurricular activities

☐ List of deadline dates
☐ Set of stamped, addressed envelopes
☐ Signed/unsigned Buckley Amendment

What would the "perfect" counselor recommendation do for you? Like a good teacher recommendation, a good counselor recommendation can support both your academic strengths and your personal interests. It can also summarize the reactions of teachers, touch on extra-curricular activities, and reinforce the ideas you express in your essay. A good counselor recommendation can provide the glue that holds together the different aspects of your application.

Supplementary Materials

From the desk of Mayor Small
Suite 1000, City Hall
(206) USA-1000

To whom it may concern:

It has come to my attention that young Andrew McAfee is applying for admission to your fine institution. Let me assure you, Andrew is a model citizen. It is my understanding that he is not only a fine student and varsity letterman but also a civic-minded member of his community. His services at the local Boys' Club in Crosstown have been exemplary.

Please feel free to call upon my staff if you have any questions.

Sincerely,
Mayor Small

Just what are supplementary materials? Are they helpful? Necessary? Wanted? Supplementary materials are any additional documents you might include with your application beyond what is required: an extra letter of recommendation, a tape of a musical performance or composition, a photograph, a piece of artwork, a literary piece, a science project, a newspaper article written by or about you.

Should you include supplementary information? Do college admissions offices really want more? What should you include? Where should you draw the line? Supplementary information serves one good purpose. It is an opportunity for you to document and describe any aspect of your life that has not and cannot be covered by the formal documents in an application.

It's a little breathing space. But keep it in perspective. This is not required material. Colleges take great pains to develop applications that ask the right questions and cover enough ground to let them make decisions about the candidates without further information. Many colleges, however, do invite you to send additional information. They made allowances for possible omissions in their applications and welcome information about aspects of your life that they would not otherwise see. But colleges do not tell you specifically what to send, and more important, they do not tell you when to stop.

In the admissions business there is good news and there is unwanted news. Be careful. There is an ancient adage: "The thicker the folder, the thicker the student." You don't want to submit an application that is so thick with clippings, summer science projects, and extra letters that it slows the discovery process of an evaluation. Folders that are two inches thick make admissions officers suspicious.

Before we suggest what you may want to include as supplementary information, let's be clear about what to avoid.

Things to Omit

- Do not include letters of recommendation from persons who do not know you personally or who do not know you very well. Avoid letters from governors, congressional representatives, or influential business people if you do not have an ongoing relationship. A friend of the family whose hand you shake once a year? Forget it. Colleges are not taken in by stationery with an impressive letterhead.

- Do not include letters of recommendation from persons who can add nothing to what has already been submitted for consideration. Extra letters of recommendation from teachers do not further your candidacy unless they add a new dimension or perspective to your application.

- Do not include documents or awards that are already mentioned in your essays or in other parts of the application. Colleges generally believe the claims that you make. You don't need to send actual proof to back up your achievements. This is not what we mean by substantiation. Awards from camp or scholastic honors can be mentioned in the format of extracurricular activities. Don't clutter your application folder with merit badges, typing certificates, or athletic association awards.

- Do not flood your folder with newspaper clippings. If you have written a lot for your school newspaper, send one or two articles. Do not send your entire portfolio. Be selective. No scrapbooks.

- Do not include term papers or scientific reports. These are troublesome to read and very often do not add anything new to your application. Remember, an admissions officer wants to learn about *you*, not about invertebrate biology or Germany between the two world wars.

Things to Include

Supplementary information is welcome whenever there is an important aspect of your life that cannot be reached by the rest of the application. Suppose you are a poet or an artist. Suppose you started a youth program through the local town council. Suppose you build racing bicycles or boats from scratch. These are all activities that you would want to document.

- Include letters of recommendation from those who are in charge of a community-based activity in which you play a substantial role. This is precisely the kind of information that a teacher recommendation or a counselor's report cannot capture: your world outside school.

- You might want to obtain a letter of recommendation from a teacher who is important to you but who does not teach an academic course (by college standards). This is where the debate or drama coach can help your candidacy. These teachers know an aspect of your life that others might not get to see.

- If you have a special or unique talent, think about how you might document this. More paper does not necessarily mean a higher level of proficiency or skill. Selected photographs or pieces of art can be submitted in the form of slides. Recitals and musical compositions can be submitted on tape. Try to send information that is easy to digest. Avoid sending tapes of musicals and plays in which you had only a small part.

A few years ago we received a cassette tape of a choir. The tape was forwarded to the music department for an evaluation. As expected, the report came back reading: "Very pretty sound. Which of the 101 singers is the applicant?" Needless to say, this did not boost the candidacy in the slightest bit.

The object is to suggest gently how serious and dedicated you are to specific outside interests. Offer the documentation necessary to drive home a point about a talent. Substantiate the bicycle with a picture. Send the blueprints of your boat design. If you are a writer, send a short story or a collection of poetry.

One of our fondest memories is of an applicant who built a balsa wood airplane to scale. He used only a penknife, wood, tissue, paper, and glue. He said that it could be outfitted with a small gasoline engine and that it could fly. A collection of Polaroid photographs accompanied the short explanation: five pictures of the airplane in various stages of design, one of the ruined plane, and one of the family dog. The dog had eaten the plane.

Bottom line: Don't feel compelled to send anything just because you have the opportunity to do so. Only when supplementary information will bring light to an important aspect of your life should you send some carefully selected information.

A Note about Sports

If you are involved in a sport at the varsity level and would like to continue to participate in college, get in touch with the athletic office at the colleges to which you are applying. Write a letter. If you run track, for example, include your times. If you play field hockey or football, include positions played and all other pertinent information. Take the initiative and communicate with the coaching staff. Include with your application a photocopy of your first letter to the coach. Cover your bases.

5

Facts
and
Myths about
Getting into
College

*E*veryone has a story. You wonder if it's true. Do the rich, the athletic, the children of alumni, the kids from North Dakota, and the privately educated really have an edge? Or worse, are they automatically admitted?

We have concentrated on the facts of the admissions process through the preceding chapters in this book. The myths, however, still need to be addressed head-on. Some are larger than life. Some are patently ridiculous. Some bear out the truth. Whether fact or fiction, most are believed.

In our travels and in our meetings with students, counselors, and parents, we were often asked, "Is it true that . . . ?" Here are some of our responses.

- *Is it true that geography is a consideration?*

Applicants rarely believe they have grown up in the right place. They think that the applicant from Oregon or Massachusetts or New Mexico has the edge, unless they happen to be from one of those states. Geography may play a role but is never going to be the only consideration.

Colleges are interested in putting together a diverse class. This means that they want to admit students with different backgrounds. Geography (where you grew up, the size of the community, the influence of an urban or a rural environment) can be helpful in telling an admissions committee what has shaped your life. The "surprise" factor is also a consideration. A college in the Northwest may be particularly interested in an unexpected applicant from the Southeast. Of course, the initial interest and curiosity will fade quickly if the student's overall qualifications are not up to par.

Colleges also use geography to measure life-styles and opportunities. Students can be expected to take advantage of only what is available to them. So don't beg your parents to move; you have had experiences and opportunities that others haven't shared. You have received advice and information from sources that don't exist elsewhere. Be aware of the opportunities your community has to offer and take advantage of them. That is what admissions committee members will look for when they build a class. Geography matters insofar as you will be sharing your experiences with other students.

- *Is it true that the children of alumni have an edge?*

There are two answers to this question: yes and no. Most colleges give the children of alumni a slight edge in the admissions process. It is important for a school to maintain ties with its graduates. The children of alumni bring tradition to the campus, and the policy helps maintain a healthy endowment. Bear in mind, however, that alumni children account for only a small percentage of each class and that many of those admitted would have been accepted without the advantage of their connection.

It is rare for a college to accept alumni children who won't be able to handle the pressure or the competition. The alumni status of parents is a consideration for public relations reasons. If a child has problems meeting the college's standards once he or she is admitted, the parents' relationship with the college may deteriorate. No one wins in such a situation.

Will your chances be hurt because your parents did not attend the college of your choice? Your credentials and your application will speak for themselves. If your candidacy is compelling, you will be admitted.

Bottom line: If one of your parents has attended or has graduated from a college to which you are applying *and* if you are a qualified and compelling applicant, you will have a slight edge. If you are a qualified and compelling applicant and neither of your parents attended the college of your choice, you will be in the same position as the majority of the other qualified applicants.

- *Is it true that some people can pay their way in?*

In these days of shrinking budgets, colleges need money. They need alumni support and contributions. Despite this great need, colleges cannot afford to grant admission to students who cannot meet their academic standards, even if the students' families are major contributors. If the son or daughter of a big contributor is in an applicant pool, the admissions committee might be aware of the high level of support and give the application close attention, but the money will not be the sole determining factor.

Colleges measure the level of alumni support in ways other than their contributing money, such as their organizing a local alumni club or sitting on a college alumni committee. Each may be a consideration. But again, it will be only a small one. As we mentioned above, if a child of a big supporter can't perform well, the relationship between the family and the college is bound to suffer.

- *Is it true that your parents' educational back-ground makes a difference?*

Colleges consider this information for reasons similar to their reasons for consideration of geography. It helps them understand your environment. The committee will make a few small assumptions from the educational background of your parents.

If your parents attended college, the admissions committee will assume that you have had at least some encouragement in the application and selection process. This assumption, however, is usually nothing more than an educated guess and plays little, if any, part in the admissions decision.

The committee will give more consideration to the fact that your parents did not attend college. While this is not a valid indication of how encouraging your parents are of your college plans, it may indicate that there was less academic support in your home. In other words, there is an assumption that you could not get help from your mom or dad on your trigonometry homework when others could. This is not a qualitative assumption, but one that the admissions committee makes in assessing the environments and opportunities that are available to you at your high school and home. It is again just one small factor in the decision. It will not help or hurt your application significantly if your parents did or did not attend college.

- *Is it true that private/public/parochial school students have an edge?*

You may have heard that students from the local private school have an easier time getting into the "top" colleges. You may wonder if colleges have quotas for students from each type of school. You may wonder if it would have been better to go to the parochial or the private school rather than the public school.

The admissions committee does not make these kinds of categorical assumptions because they understand that a school can only be as good as its students, faculty, and administration. Each school is looked at separately. The applicants are judged both individually and as members of their own particular school environment.

Colleges look at a high school to determine what challenges are afforded its students, what extracurricular activities are available, what upper-level courses are offered, and what community it serves. These factors can't be found in a label. Admissions officers visit high schools; they speak with alumni. Counselors may indicate whether this year's group is particularly strong or weak. Each of these factors will color the admissions office's opinion of a particular school and this particular class.

The committee will not need to make inaccurate assumptions based only on a label.

- *Is it true that there is a quota for each high school?*

There are no quotas. There are rates of admission that will tell you that not everyone applying to a college will get in. This rate of admission, however, is not applied to each group of applicants from each school. If the applicants from your high school are particularly strong, the admissions committee won't hesitate to admit above the national average. After all, that's what it is—an average. There will be other schools in the country with a particularly weak group of applicants from which no one will be admitted or where the rate will fall below the national average.

The admissions committee will probably make some comparisons among the applicants from a school. It helps them understand what courses are available and, more generally, what the school offers its students.

Don't base your choice of colleges on the choices of those who are above you in class rank. Class rank will be only one of many considerations. It's not an accurate predictor of the success of the other candidates from your class. Those who rely on it will be surprised unless, of course, a college admits on the basis of class rank or percentile alone.

Each year some colleges reject valedictorians at schools from which they accept other students. Make your own choices and present your case as strongly as possible. A successful application comes from concentrating on the choices you have made and the ideas you have, rather than on the fates of your classmates and fellow applicants.

- *Is it true that students who apply from schools where there have been many offers of admission, or many applicants in the past, have an advantage?*

There are two fictions here. The first derives from the mistaken assumption that a college "doesn't like" the applicants from your high school; or worse, the college doesn't like your high school, period. The second is based on another mistaken assumption—that the college knows nothing about your high school and therefore is unwilling to accept any applicants from it.

Unless you're exactly like other applicants from your high school who have been denied admission, their rejections shouldn't affect your chance of admission or your choice of colleges. Each applicant is looked at as an individual, apart from other applicants, successful or unsuccessful. The previous track record of applicants from your school has no bearing on your application.

If you carefully research the history of the relationship between your high school and each college to which you're applying, you might find it quirky. One year the valedictorian was rejected; the next, a student with lower rank was admitted. One year three of five applicants were admitted; the next, all applicants were rejected. Remember that a college builds a new class each year—its needs, class balance, and scope of the applicant pool change. Any trend that you might see could have developed for many reasons: one or two colleges could be immensely popular. This popularity will result in a large number of applicants, many of whom will be unrealistic. This previous or present deluge will skew the statistics.

A college may also have an inaccurate reputation among students at your school. We recall a complaint from a fellow admissions officer whose college received from a particular high school only those applicants whose statistics fell way below the college's national average. Somehow the students at this high school had received the impression that it was a "sure-thing" college. These misconceptions are easily corrected with research.

But what about the valedictorians who were rejected in the past few years? A valedictorian can write a dull essay, can choose the wrong teachers to write recommendations, or can do a poor job putting together an application. Don't make the same mistakes. Reverse the trend.

89

What if there is no trend, good or bad? What if no one has applied from your high school in the past 10 years, or ever? There are many ways a college can obtain information about your high school. Your application will tell them a great deal from the transcript, the statistics on class size, and the activities in which you have been involved. Many schools send a profile that is filled with this kind of helpful information. An admissions officer who is confused by a policy or a program, or simply needs to know more, will get in touch with your counselor or an alumus in the area who is familiar with your school.

Colleges are aware of their own limitations. You won't be penalized because their admissions staffs can't travel to every high school in the country this year, or any year. Colleges develop their applications with these limitations in mind. They ask questions that will give them a glimpse of your world. One other consideration is the advantage you may enjoy as the only applicant from your high school in many years. That will set you apart because the admissions office may wonder how you ever heard of its college or what prompted you to apply after the long dry spell. There are advantages to being first.

- *It is true that athletes have an advantage?*

A winning football team means bigger alumni contributions for many colleges. Winning teams produce revenue, but an athlete, like all other applicants, will be evaluated as a whole person. It won't help an athletic program to have athletes admitted who become ineligible because of academic probation. Athletics certainly will be one of the pluses in the application and will earn it close scrutiny, but there will have to be other strengths as well.

In the class of students who are admitted, there will be students with strengths that are more visible than others. These are the classmates you will see on the athletic field, in the concert hall, or on the stage. But their achievements are no more noteworthy or weighty than

90

those of the students who excel in the classroom, in the community, or on the intramural field. A diverse class will naturally contain students who represent various gifts and achievements.

What about the support of coaches? If you're planning to play a varsity sport, it is a good idea to get in touch with the appropriate coach, who will assess your ability and tell the admissions committee how you would contribute to the athletic program. This is really no different from the assessments that the admissions committee makes about the talents and strengths of each of the students admitted. The committee defers to the judgment of a coach as to athletic skills but does not admit on the basis of this recommendation alone. Similar discussions occur between the music or English departments and the admissions offices when a tape or creative writing sample is sent. The committee simply turns to an expert for an opinion on the talents of a student in a specialized area. When it makes its decision, an admissions office will consider the opinion rendered along with all the other parts of an application.

The
Big
Picture

"Okay, I understand the purpose of each of these pieces of paper. I think I may even have a topic for my essay. It might even be fun to write. I have narrowed down my teachers to three possibilities. I wonder whether my senior math teacher or my sophomore bio teacher will do a better job. I even got a chance to talk with my counselor, but I'm still not sure how all of this will come across. I want to be likable but not saccharine. I want to appear committed but not myopic. There are so many impressions that I'd like to leave with them. But I want to appear focused. Mostly, I just want to get in."

Your Application as a Whole

After you understand the purpose of each individual document, it's important to consider the big picture—how your application will appear as a whole. With such a limited space, you want to be sure that each document conveys a message. If one of your teacher recommendations falls short, if the teacher is straining to find something to say about you, a crucial page will be wasted.

Make a list of the documents and try to predict what each will communicate to the admissions committee. What aspects of your high school record (academic and extracurricular) will each document highlight? What will each say about you as a person? That's more difficult to predict but worth considering. If you ask for a recommendation from a history teacher who is also the adviser to the student council, of which you are president, it's fairly predictable the teacher will talk about your leadership skills. On the other hand, if you've chosen someone who teaches a course that focuses on writing, with little class discussion, it's fairly certain the teacher will mention your writing prowess but may not know a lot about you personally.

It should be easy to imagine what information the committee will derive from your essay. As the author, you are in control of the essay. If you think that your essay takes some risks and may not leave the impression you hoped for, be optimistic. The admissions committee responds positively to essays that do more than state the obvious.

You should also consider the academic documents: the transcript and your test scores. Each will indicate your academic ability and achievements but will also shed light on the breadth and depth of your academic career. These statistics speak for themselves but are easily augmented by other documents.

Once you make your predictions, you need to think about what's missing. You must consider what aspect of your life hasn't been highlighted and whether there are inconsistencies or redundancies. Two documents shouldn't say exactly the same thing, but some repetition is acceptable and, depending on your game plan, important.

It is imperative for each document to have a purpose. Don't solicit a recommendation from your sophomore English teacher if you think it will be superfluous. It is frustrating to think that important decisions are made with what seems like so little information about you. Don't waste the chance to give more.

Your goal in creating this list of documents is to realize what your application will ultimately say. When you consider your application and the impression it will leave, you may find it helpful to think about two application models: the multi-interest application and the focused-interest application. These models exemplify how a collection of documents can paint a big picture. They are general types, not hard-and-fast categories. Your application might easily fall in between. If so, consider the approach of both, and apply what is appropriate to your interests.

The Multi-Interest Application

The biggest problem for someone with lots of different interests and activities is to cover them all while developing a theme or focus in the application. If you do many things well, that may be a theme in itself. It is still necessary, however, to consider who will talk about which strengths.

When you choose your essay topic, think about areas that no one else will be able to cover. Think of the information teachers and counselors have and what they lack. If you are devoted to a community activity and no one in school is aware of your participation, you may want to talk about it in your essay. Don't expect a teacher recommendation to highlight an activity when the teacher's first

notice of your involvement comes from the list of extra-curriculars you prepared. To convey an interest fully, the person talking about it should have firsthand knowledge.

What if no one at school knows of your interests and there are too many activities to include in an essay for fear of its becoming a list? This is where supplementary materials make perfect sense. Be creative. Supplementary material need not be recommendations, although some-times they are the most obvious and appropriate choice. You can also submit slides or tapes. In any case, as you consider your list of documents, remember that supple-mentary materials can be useful backups, as long as you submit them selectively.

A connecting theme is often difficult to establish in the multi-interest application. Sometimes there really isn't one. By now you may feel that the theme in your life is anxiety over college and weariness of the application process. Take the time to consider how you spend your time. Is there a connecting motivation in what you do? A theme can be as obvious as love of the arts or community service and as subtle as always being a sidekick or the one to add a little humor to any situation. If there is a theme that you'd like the admissions committee to notice, make sure it appears in your application.

Probably the most difficult place to express the theme is in the essay. True, the essay is a natural place to put something that can't be found anywhere else, but describing a theme is difficult. First, it is hard not to sound contrived and prepackaged. It is also difficult to stay clear of making your essay into a list when you must support your contention that there's a theme to your life. You might successfully explain how two of your interests connect, but when you try to fit in four or five, the task becomes more complicated.

Again, you'll need to rely on what others have to say about you. Don't sell teachers and counselors short. If they've watched your high school career, they've probably developed their own impressions and may comment on the themes they see as connecting your interests and talents. You may want to help them by grouping what you see as thematic interests on the extracurricular sheet you give to them.

The admissions committee will also come to its own conclusions. As we mentioned earlier, a diverse group of developed interests often creates its own theme. Many times at the committee table, we were asked to talk about a student's focus. After we mentioned three or four commitments, the committee was satisfied that we had an applicant who made an impact in high school and was therefore someone who would have an impact at Yale. Sometimes it was hard to predict exactly where, but clearly this was a student who would not sit back while others became involved or took action. That reassurance was enough.

This assumption is not reached, however, from a list. When you consider how you'll use each document, make sure that the activities and interests you want emphasized are brought to life by you or others in your application.

The multi-interest application has a natural theme: you and what makes you tick. Not only should each of your interests appear somewhere in the application, but there should be a sense of priority to the arrangement as well. A multi-interest application will appear unfocused if it doesn't make clear what is most important to you. You may not be able to narrow it down to one interest, but you should decide which few interests should be prominent.

Let two teachers cover different areas of involvement. If you are a student with several important interests, the committee will enjoy hearing from teachers who have worked with you in different contexts. But don't rely on teacher recommendations to cover all the bases: that's your job.

Consistency becomes an important consideration when you are aligning your priorities. If your list of extracurricular activities indicates that athletics is your first priority and everyone else mentions your activity in the community, the committee will begin to wonder about the inconsistency. But how about getting everything in? The key is to be truthful in your assessment of your priorities; it will then be more likely that teachers will comment about activities that are consistent with what you've said about yourself. A theme cannot be created where none exists. Just as your essay and extracurricular list must truly reflect your thoughts and interests, any theme you choose to develop must be a true reflection of your high school career.

What is important is that you consider your application as a whole and think about how well it represents you. A true reflection, well and thoughtfully presented, will be the most illuminating.

The Focused-Interest Application

In considering the big picture, if you have focused and excelled in one area—academic or extracurricular—you will have an easier time developing a theme. It's right there for you in the energy and commitment involved in that one interest. Your job will be to make sure the committee understands not only the extent of your commitment but also why you have chosen to focus, why you have devoted yourself to that one interest to the exclusion of others. It may seem obvious to you, but to someone who has not shared your excitement, it can sometimes prove difficult to understand.

The easiest place to describe these motivations is in your essay. Too many students who have excelled in one area use their essay to list awards they've won or to detail the history of their development in that area, which results in a factual and usually tedious account. These lists are more effective elsewhere. The essay is your chance to describe the emotions that accompany both the triumphs and the failures. It should be a subjective description, not a factual one.

If there are two essays, both should probably not be written on the same topic. The committee will be curious to see what you've done with the opportunity to discuss something other than your central interest.

You may be the best musician, athlete, writer, or student ever to graduate from your high school, but in a national applicant pool you will probably be one of many. Don't sell yourself short, but remember that you will have competition, perhaps for the first time. Don't rest on your laurels. Let the committee see beyond your talents to the person whom they will admit. The admissions committee is going to admit a person, not just a musician, an athlete, or a mathematician. They will welcome your talents and contributions on their campus but will also think of you as a roommate and classmate to the others who are admitted.

You should also consider this single interest when you are choosing the teachers who will write your recommendations. If you believe that your artistic strengths warrant your admission, comments from teachers who taught you in a more traditional classroom setting might also be appropriate and helpful (if not required). The admissions committee wants to know that your talent is truly special but also needs to measure your strengths in other areas. You don't have to show them your weaknesses, but you should give them a sense of how you'll handle other demands of college life.

If you are ready for a change, or have other interests that have been gnawing at the back of your mind, mention them. You shouldn't be afraid that the admissions committee will view your digressions as disloyalty or lack of interest. At your age, no one will want you to sign on the dotted line, guaranteeing that you'll play for four years in the orchestra or on the volleyball team. Your dedication will be apparent in your accomplishments.

You should also consider soliciting recommendations from teachers who are aware of your accomplishments and commitments. If you leave school every day to attend four hours of dance rehearsal, it would help the committee to hear from someone who is in a position to comment on how that commitment has affected your work in other areas and maybe even your relationship with your classmates.

Although the focused-interest application will have a natural theme, it will require some careful thought about documentation and depth. While members of the admissions committee are essentially looking at one interest to describe you, it is crucial that they are able to connect the interest to you as a person. Make them understand your passion, and you will give them a fuller sense of why that interest has consumed your time.

Does Your Application Say It All?

Again, these are just two general models. By reading about each, you should have some idea of what to consider when looking at your application in its entirety. Remember that those few pieces of paper will be responsible for everything the admissions committee knows about you. Don't rely on anyone else to get that information to the committee.

Think about the results. Imagine two or three persons reading your application. Would you be satisfied with what they'd know about you and, more important, what they wouldn't know? If you are disappointed by the results, if you feel that there's a chunk missing, then think about how you could fit that in. The application can say as much or as little as you allow.

If there is something missing, don't automatically rely on supplementary material. Consider whether that information could be included somewhere in the forms provided by the college. If you think these are inadequate, consider using supplementary material.

If you're happy with your essay, keep it the way it is. But if it seems to you that the application does not convey the sense of the person behind it, that it would fail to draw in the admissions committee, you should take another look at your essay. The essay is not the place to fill in factual gaps. Those can be filled by choosing a teacher with the right information or by simply rearranging or adding to your list of extracurricular activities.

Now is also the time to consider what you have done to help counter distractingly low test scores or problematic slips on your transcript. These criteria can be supplemented and even offset by comments from your teachers and counselor. The admissions committee will put more faith in the opinion of someone who has seen your skills applied in the classroom than in the tests that are supposed to measure those skills. They won't ignore test results or the weak spots on your transcript, but they will listen to the comments of someone who has worked with you for a semester, quarter, or year, rather than one Saturday morning.

Suggestions—Not Rules

Here's one last piece of advice, which may sound rather ironic in light of what we've written so far: don't overplan. This book is full of suggestions, not rules. It's full of our ideas about what might help you better understand the admissions process. By no means are we advocating that every application be either multi-interest or focused-interest, or that everyone need follow the five-day plan.

As you have probably noticed, a recurring theme is that you have to be yourself, that the best representation is a true representation. You will only be able to impress the committee with your individuality if you leave in some spontaneity along with the consistency. Don't plan the fun, the surprise, and the quirks out of your application.

7

Special
Situations

Students Graduating Early
from High School

Every year colleges receive applications from students who have fulfilled their graduation requirements ahead of schedule. If you are one of those students who have exhausted their high school curriculum by the end of the eleventh grade (or before), you might find yourself applying to colleges in your junior year (or earlier).

It is important to remember that your education consists of more than just academics. Colleges, when they admit you, want to be certain that you will be able to adapt to a rigorous academic environment and survive the mayhem of a class of 18-year-olds struggling to find themselves. Colleges will be concerned about various aspects of your social maturity—how well you interact with both your peers and your teachers and how well you adapt to a change of environment.

One way colleges evaluate your social maturity is by considering your participation in extracurricular activities. As we have mentioned, your involvement in these activities reveals to admissions officers such qualities as your leadership skills and potential, your ability to get along with others, and your concern for the community.

Some of these qualities manifest themselves, to a degree, in the classroom, but they tend to develop more freely in an extracurricular setting. Extracurricular activities can involve interacting with people in ways that the classroom just will not allow. Whether it is sports, music, or journalism, whether it takes place in your school or in the community, an extracurricular activity allows you to explore yourself and express yourself, to discover hidden talents you might not otherwise have found.

For better or worse, most extracurricular activities operate on a seniority basis. In many high schools it is difficult to obtain a senior position on the newspaper, a captaincy of a sport, or the vice presidency of the student council unless you are a senior and have participated in the activity for some time. Such opportunities do not so readily present themselves to juniors or sophomores. We do not mean that you must hold an office of some kind to gain acceptance to college. We do mean that commitment to a certain activity over an extended period of time will result in more responsibility. And admissions officers like to admit people who can handle responsibility.

So, if you are applying to college after only two or three years in high school, you may find it a challenge to demonstrate your social maturity and readiness for college to an admissions committee. You may not have had the opportunity to let your leadership qualities shine through. Had you stayed another year or two, you could have been class president—but colleges won't know this unless you tell them.

If you apply early, your goal should be to present the admissions committee with as compelling a case as possible on the personal side. Chances are, if you are graduating early, your case will already be compelling on the academic side. The academics will speak for themselves; now you must speak for yourself.

Remember the control you have over the application and use that control to your advantage. Take extra care to give your recommendation forms to teachers who can speak to your personal qualities as well as your academic strengths. Make sure your guidance counselor knows the extent to which you have participated in extracurricular activities, whether they are in school or out. Think about the role your essays can play in revealing to an admissions committee your personal strengths and maturity.

Students Who Have Attended
More than One High School

Many applicants will have attended more than one high school by the time they complete the twelfth grade. For example, we read a number of applications from children of parents who had jobs that required a move every year. Other cases were less extreme. There may have been only one move—and it occurred directly after the student had completed the ninth grade.

There is a general rule to follow here to ensure that your application best describes you: the more recent the change in schools, the more you should think about obtaining supporting documents from more than one school. As we have mentioned, you should solicit recommendations from teachers who have taught you recently and who know you well. When you switch schools, transcripts and test scores are usually forwarded from school to school automatically. Teachers' impressions and comments are not.

In other words, if you moved at the end of the ninth grade and have been at the same school ever since, there is probably no need to request recommendations from your old school. If, on the other hand, you will be spending your senior year at a new school, you should consider submitting two sets of teacher recommendations and two sets of counselor recommendations, one from your old school and one from the new.

In chapter 4 we advised you against submitting too many recommendations, but we retract our advice for this special case. Most colleges will appreciate both sets of recommendations, which will provide them with a better sense of your capabilities than will either set alone. If you have spent three years at one school, the personnel there know you best. They know you participated in drama, that you were a valuable contributor to the swim team, and that you were a vital force in school government. They are able to relate specific anecdotes about you.

Use your best judgment. If you have just moved to a new school for your last year, teachers and counselors at this new school obviously do not know you as well as do those at your old school. If you had a favorite tenth-grade teacher at another school, write to that teacher and ask for a recommendation.

When asking teachers at a previous school to write recommendations for you, be sure to bring them up-to-date on your current situation and be sure to include stamped, addressed envelopes so the teachers can mail their comments directly to the colleges. Make their task as easy as possible.

What impact will switching schools have on your class rank and involvement in extracurricular activities? How will admissions officers react to such changes? As we mentioned in chapter 2, not all schools calculate class rank in the same fashion; it is likely, if you change schools, that your new school will figure class rank differently from your old one. Depending on the new school's ranking policy, this can have either a deleterious or a positive effect on your old rank.

Anne, who switched schools after the eleventh grade, received a B in honors biology in the tenth grade. Although her old school gave added weight to honors courses when calculating class rank, the new school in which she enrolled does not give extra weight to honors courses. As a result, her rank could conceivably be lower at the new school.

You should not worry too much about such adjustments to your class rank. Admissions officers are savvy enough to realize that if you switch schools, your class rank can be affected. Remember that admissions officers look at the transcript as a whole; they scrutinize your grades and the difficulty of your courses. Though class rank can provide a useful "snapshot" of your transcript, in some cases it cannot. Be assured that an admissions officer will be sensitive to your situation and will hunt down the reasons for any dramatic increase or decrease in your class standing.

Changing schools can also affect your participation in extracurricular activities. If you played soccer for the first three years of high school and then transferred to a school that doesn't field a soccer team, your soccer career could end. What if you were carefully cultivating supporters for a run for president of the student body and were forced to move to a different school just before the election?

Obviously, admissions officers cannot expect miracles. We know that switching schools can be as grueling as it is refreshing. While you look forward to making new friends and meeting new people, there always is the tension associated with having to become familiar with a strange place and, of course, the anxiety that accompanies leaving behind old friends and familiar routines. Such emotions are inevitable, but if you can transform them into a positive force, so much the better. Participate eagerly and enthusiastically in activities that come your way.

A proven ability to assimilate into a new environment both academically and socially will tell admissions officers that you will fare well when you make the move from high school to college.

Deferred-Admissions Students

Some students will consider taking off a year or two between high school and college either to earn money to defray the costs of college tuition, or to see the world. These students are faced with important decisions: is it better to apply to colleges during the senior year and seek deferred enrollment, or is it better to wait and apply when ready to enroll?

Your decision to take time off will depend on many factors: your financial situation, your choices and opportunities, and your certainty about college. The decision is yours. But once your decision has been made, how should you approach the college application process?

There are some obvious advantages to applying to colleges during the fall of your senior year. A high school guidance office is best prepared to work with enrolled students. Transcripts are available, report cards are easily retrievable, and counselors know you and carry your files as their responsibility. You are in the midst of continuing relationships with your teachers. They know you, you know them. The key word here is accessibility.

If you wait a year or two before beginning the application process, you do not have the advantage of that routine access to teachers and counselors. School records have to be retrieved from files. Teachers you want to ask for recommendations have taught lots of other students since your time and may not recall in detail your accomplishments and classroom contributions. Guidance counselors have to make special efforts to provide you with help. Even worse, teachers and guidance counselors who know you may have left the school by the time you are ready to apply.

If you apply during your senior year for deferred enrollment, how will that affect the college's admissions decision? The best way to get an accurate answer is to ask each college about its policy. Some colleges welcome applications from students who wish to defer enrollment. Some even provide a check box on the application form itself that gives you an opportunity to declare such an intent.

At the other extreme are colleges that will not review applications from students who wish to defer. These colleges are concerned with admitting qualified applicants

112

for enrollment the following fall (not just admitting applicants who, one day, might decide to enroll). Obviously, many colleges fall somewhere in between. Their policies are flexible, and when students present compelling reasons for deferred enrollment, a committee will make decisions on a case-by-case basis.

Our advice is this. If a college will not consider your application for deferred enrollment or if you choose not to apply to college while you are in high school, take advantage of the opportunities that exist to gather information. Ask teachers to write recommendations for you and have these recommendations stored in your school file along with your transcript. Make a list of your extracurricular activities for your school or personal file. Ask your guidance counselor to write a report and to keep it with all your other assembled papers. If you explain your plan to the guidance counselor, he or she can give you advice and help in dealing with this situation. Remember, it is always easier for a teacher or guidance counselor to recall and discuss the academic and personal qualities of a present student.

Foreign Students*

Many colleges welcome applications from foreign students and depend on them to make their campuses more diverse and thereby more interesting. Admissions procedures are generally the same for foreign students and citizens of the United States, but there are a few noteworthy exceptions of which you should be aware. We outline below the steps you should take to ensure that your application receives the best possible consideration.

*We define foreign students as non-American citizens living in the United States (as permanent or nonpermanent residents) or abroad.

Conveying English Proficiency— The TOEFL and Your Essay

In addition to requesting the SAT or ACT, most colleges require students whose native language is not English to take the Test of English as a Foreign Language (TOEFL), which is administered by Educational Testing Service under the auspices of the College Board and the Graduate Record Examination Board. The TOEFL consists of three separate sections. The first, Listening Comprehension, measures your ability to understand spoken English. The second, Structure and Written Expression, measures your ability to recognize standard written English. The third, Vocabulary and Reading Comprehension, measures your ability to understand everyday reading material.

Many colleges have a minimum TOEFL score below which applicants will not be admitted. On request, colleges will advise you what that minimum level of proficiency is. Most minimum scores fall in the 500-to-600 range on a 0-to-800 scale. Such minimums are used to screen out those students who would find it too difficult to communicate effectively in an English-language classroom setting.

Some colleges also have a two-step application process to aid in the screening effort. First, you submit TOEFL scores and some information about your academic background. Based on this information, the college will then advise you whether or not to complete the application process.

Your essays provide admissions committees with another opportunity to assess your English writing and verbal abilities. These essays should be written by *you*— that is, with as little help as possible from others. Only in this way can admissions officers assess your true capabilities. After all, you would not want to misrepresent your abilities only to arrive on a college campus months later

114

and find that you can't comprehend the classroom discussion or handle the assignments.

When it comes to deciding what subject to write about in your essay, avoid the temptation to describe in general terms either the political situation in your country or your travels. Admissions officers can read such information in the newspaper or a travel brochure. You should feel free to write about how political events or your travels have affected you personally. Just remember, the essay is the vehicle through which admissions officers get to know you.

Providing Information about Your School

Being a foreigner can make you an attractive candidate. Try not to diminish that attraction by making your folder difficult for an admissions committee to understand. You must work a little harder than the average American applicant to make sure that your transcript can readily be understood by admissions officers in the United States. There is great variance in grading systems from country to country, and even from school to school within a particular country. A grade of 20 in one Italian school might indicate superior achievement, whereas in the United States, such a grade would most likely indicate failure.

Make it easy for admissions officers to become acquainted with both the educational system in your country and the academic and extracurricular environment at your school. It is imperative for your guidance counselor or headmaster to include a profile, a fully detailed letter, or even a school catalog along with your transcript. Ideally, any one of these documents would cover the following information:

- A description of the educational system in your country, providing answers to such questions as

How many students have access to primary, secondary, and higher education? For how many days per year and for how many hours per day do students attend classes?

- A description of the grading system and the content of any nationally or locally administered secondary school examinations you have taken.

- A detailed description of your school and its grading system, including information about how class rank is calculated. If the school does not rank its students, there should be some indication of a grade distribution—a chart showing how many times various grades or honors are awarded or an estimation of your place in the class.

- A description of the curriculum. Course titles alone do not always reveal what you have been taught in the classroom. A course entitled Topics in Mathematics, for example, could mean that you learned anything from arithmetic to the calculus of several variables.

Financial Aid

It is likely that at most colleges financial aid policies for foreign students will differ significantly from those for American citizens. Money from the United States government is awarded only to American citizens or permanent residents of the United States. As a result, it is very expensive for colleges to fund the aid packages of foreign students whose needs must be met with private funds from the colleges themselves. Because of shrinking aid budgets and a sense of first obligation to American students, there is often only limited funding available for foreign students.

The ability to finance your own education thus becomes a requirement for admission to many colleges. You should research thoroughly each college's policy with regard to funding foreign students' financial aid.

Leaving Secondary School Early

The number of years of secondary education in some foreign countries exceeds that in the United States. In the province of Ontario, Canada, for example, students normally attend high school through grade 13 before continuing on to higher education. In general you will be able to submit a more compelling application if you remain enrolled in secondary school until its natural completion. We have outlined some reasons for this in the first section of this chapter. Often you will receive advanced credit for extra work done. It is best to ask the colleges what their past experience has been with applicants from your country or region.

A General Reminder

If you live abroad, you must allow for the fact that international mails can be painfully slow. Begin your inquiries in the summer or early fall of the year in which you plan to apply to college. Mail your applications weeks before the deadlines in order to ensure full consideration of your candidacy.

Returning Students

With the high price of a college education today, it is no wonder that some students decide to postpone their entrance to college. They take jobs that allow them both the exposure to employment and the opportunity to put away some cash for their college years. Other students may have graduated from high school without the slightest intention of pursuing higher education, but their constellation of circumstances is such that a college education is now a priority.

As an older applicant (at many colleges you will be referred to as a nontraditional student, but don't let that term put you off), you face the task of persuading an admissions committee that you possess both the capability and the motivation for doing college work. Though high school students have the same task, they don't have to exert as much effort. They are now enrolled in school, where teachers and counselors are able to assess their progress. While there is no guarantee that they will live up to their teachers' praise in college, it is easier for admissions officers to make the leap of faith in their case than in yours. Why? Because people change over time, and returning to formal study after a prolonged absence can be difficult. Even with a good secondary school record, there is no guarantee, in the minds of admissions personnel, that you will perform at the same level in college years later. Because you have been away from the academic life, your performance as a high school student becomes less relevant and your high school transcript will receive less weight than it would if you were currently enrolled in high school.

You will have an easier time convincing an admissions committee of your present capabilities—and you will help admissions officers make that leap of faith—if you have taken courses recently. Grades and recommendations from teachers in those courses will play a more significant role in the admissions decision than will those of your high school years. They better reflect what you can do now.

If you have not taken any classes recently, it is probable that you will be unable to solicit recommendations from academic teachers. Your employers then will take the place of the teachers, and their recommendations can often be helpful to the committee in assessing your ability to contribute to, and survive at, college. If at all possible, whoever is writing your recommendation should discuss your intellectual ability.

Standardized testing may play a more significant role in your admissions decision than it does for regular high school applicants, especially if there is no current course work on which to base an admissions decision. In the absence of recent grades, recent test scores provide admissions officers with the next best way of assessing your academic capabilities.

A good way to prove yourself ready to attend college, to demonstrate your motivation to an admissions office, is with an interview. Many colleges require that nontraditional students meet with a member of the faculty or admissions staff. The purpose of such an interview may be purely informational: the admissions officer will give you advice about what the particular college has to offer you. Or, the interview may be purely evaluative: the admissions officer will attempt to assess your capabilities and motivation for going to college. In most cases it is both; the admissions officer acts as counselor and evaluator.

At colleges that do not require interviews, you might consider asking for one. Some applicants are very persuasive and effective in an interview. The worst an admissions office can do is to turn down your request.

Finally, and perhaps most important, your essay should describe your motivation. There is no substitute for lucid, clear prose and a compelling reason for returning to academe. Try not to make your essay a travelogue of your experiences since graduating from high school. You should submit a detailed résumé for this purpose. Use the essay to describe your reasoning. Discuss, perhaps, how further education will enhance your personal and professional goals.

Students Reapplying to College

If you tried unsuccessfully to gain admission to the college of your choice and decide to reapply to that college as an entering freshman (that is, not as a transfer student), you should know that most colleges will request that you submit a new application—new essays, recommendations, and so forth.

If you think about it, submitting an application similar to the one you submitted previously will not be to your advantage. You did not persuade the admissions committee to admit you on the first try, and unless there has been some sort of dramatic shift in admissions policy or change in the quality of the applicant pool at that particular college, you probably will not be admitted with a similar set of credentials. (Bear in mind that the committee will very likely have access to your previous application.)

Your goal, therefore, should be to capitalize on your experiences since graduating from high school, whether they involve work experience, travel, or further education. Let your essay show the admissions committee how you have grown through these experiences.

You might also think about soliciting recommendations from those who have not written for you previously. Someone whom you have met in the intervening year or years may be able to shed new light on your academic capabilities and personal qualities.

Transfer Students

If you are applying to transfer from one college to another, much of what we have addressed in the preceding chapters still applies. There are, however, some essential differences of which you should be aware.

First, your academic performance in college will take precedence over that in high school. Though most colleges to which you apply as a transfer student will request a copy of your high school transcript, that collection of grades will be superseded by those in college. An

uneven high school transcript, for example, will often become less meaningful in the presence of a compelling college transcript.

The task you have before you as a transfer applicant, which freshman applicants do not have, is to present a convincing reason for transferring to the college to which you are applying. This might require a little more work in tailoring your application to each of the colleges. With only part of your college career remaining, the admissions committee will want to be certain that you'll find a niche easily.

Your essay is as good a place as any to start, and, in fact, most colleges that request an essay will ask you to reveal your motivation for transfer. When writing your essay, don't deprecate your experience at your current institution. Concentrate instead on what you hope to gain from, and contribute to, the new college. Criticism usually does not go over well. It can make you seem bitter, even negative. You are much better off casting information in a positive light. The physics major who is disenchanted with the paucity of physics courses at the current college can always say, "I seem to have exhausted my opportunities in physics" instead of, "They didn't have enough physics courses."

Admissions committees tend to respond most favorably to those applicants who wish to transfer for substantial academic reasons: a particular professor with whom they wish to study, a particular major that exists at one college but not another, advanced courses in a subject. Transferring to another college because you think the campus is prettier, though it may be true, will not impress an admissions committee.

Your application becomes even more credible and compelling when your professors, in their recommendations, back up your reasoning for transfer. If your physics professor believes that your current college is unable to meet your needs in physics and that another college would suit you better, you will have created a consistent picture that an admissions committee may find hard to resist.

Wait-Listed Students

Any selective college, by definition, will have more applicants than spaces available in the freshman class. All these colleges will admit more students than they are able to enroll. They know that, inevitably, some students who are accepted will choose to attend other institutions. If a college underestimates the number of students who will decline its offer of admission, spaces become available, and the college looks to its waiting list of candidates in order to fill the vacancies.

Some colleges rank the students on the waiting list. In other words, if a space becomes available, the admissions committee has predetermined the first person to fill the vacancy. Other colleges are more flexible. If, for example, a tuba player turns down an offer of admission from State University, then State might decide to accept another tuba player.

Still other colleges admit students based on their continued enthusiasm. If there are 50 persons on the waiting list and four vacancies arise, the committee might accept four applicants who have communicated that the college remains their first choice. If you find yourself on the waiting list, write a follow-up letter. This letter should be rather informal and most definitely upbeat. It should outline your interest in the college and describe any accomplishments that have occurred since you submitted your application.

If you have questions about whether a college ranks its waiting list, call the admissions office. Ask to speak with the admissions officer who handled your case. Ask if the waiting list is ranked and, if so, where you stand. Talk about your enthusiasm for the college.

There is, though, a line to be drawn between demonstrating enthusiasm and being a pest. Admissions officers tend to react negatively to a deluge of information and letters and phone calls from the secretary of state, the governor, your father's best friend, and your grandmother. You might consider, however, sending an extra letter of recommendation from a teacher who has not previously written for you. If the teacher knows you well, this could give you an added boost. Remember, show your interest but keep the pestering to a minimum.

Getting
Ready
for the
Send-Off

here are only two important ideas left to consider: time and faith. No, this is not a last-minute lecture in philosophy or religion. It is a discussion of two crucial concepts that you must keep with you throughout the application process.

Give Yourself Time

Everyone tells you to plan. Make a chart. Mark a calendar. That is not our message. We do not insist that your essay be typed and proofread at least 10 days before you intend to mail your applications. We ask only that you consider time.

Time is important because it invites perspective. When you have time, you have a chance to think and to reflect. When you have time, you have free moments to examine the choices you have made.

Time, therefore, does not mean marks on your school planner. Time means the flexibility to think, to plan, and to change your mind. The time for this introspection is not the eleventh hour before an application must be postmarked.

Our message is simple: Now that you have read this book, leave yourself plenty of time to think about the many ideas we have given you. Think about the big picture. Think about what information is already in the application and what information you need to provide. Think about all the options you will want to consider before you act. Save time for these deliberations. You can use time to your advantage.

Have Faith in Yourself

Faith readily translates into an inner strength or a belief in yourself. The application process is rarely fun.

Someone is asking you to reveal yourself through words on paper and to characterize your achievements in a manner that will compel an admissions board to accept you.

There will be times when you will think yourself pretty ordinary. There will be times when you feel humbled or even beaten.

If you can remember your dreams and your passions and the choices that you have made and followed, the application cannot defeat you. If you can remember that you are the compendium of 17 years of experience, education, and interaction, you will be able to do the job.

This is faith. It is a recognition of your achievements. If you can keep this feeling of strength with you, you will do fine. Let this sense of security, this fundamental pride, guide you.

Our work is over and yours must begin. We hope that you have learned from this book and enjoyed reading it. It is written just for you—not for your parents and not for your teachers. Please do not leave this book on a shelf. Thumb through it before an interview or before you hand over your teacher recommendation forms. Refer to the Contents or Index when you want to reread a particular piece of information or advice.

While we have given you lots of suggestions about how to approach your college applications, we have not given you many absolutes or instructions to follow blindly. As you have read, you have interpreted the information, picked particular suggestions to remember, and chosen certain styles that made sense to you.

Follow these inclinations. Think about the message you want to get across. Take the time to reflect on your many achievements and idiosyncracies. Have the faith to talk openly about both your strengths and your weaknesses.

At a certain point you should have the confidence to stop. You will be ready to put on the stamp, check your social security number once more, and lick the envelope.

When you reach that point, be satisfied with your effort and take a relaxed, easy walk to the nearest mailbox.

Good luck!

Index